FLIP YA LIFE

Eric "Shabazz The OG" Lowe

As told to
Tiffany Muller

FLIP YA LIFE

Dedication

This book is dedicated primarily to my immediate family. My mother, Rosalind, who is the very reason the morals, values and integrity that I stand upon were instilled in me. My Grandmother, Louise Appling, who is the first person that showed me what it is to have unconditional love, whether right, wrong or indifferent. I want to thank Mr. Richard, as well, for making my mother happy.

Also, to my Father, Bobby Hamilton, who, although despite an estranged relationship growing up, through him as an adult I was able to understand things as a man about manhood that I didn't understand as a child.

To my siblings: Kevin – My little "Big" brother and my young "Old Head". I looked up to you, homie and you didn't even know it. To my baby brother Kirby – my unofficial twin and definition of all little brothers; you owe me a Polo jacket. Kim – The protector of all protectors. No! I'm not moving back to Philly, I'm good in Miami. To Baby Erica – If ever you need me you know I'll come; ready to kill with a smokin' gun. You know what it is. My baby sister Elesha – You're probably the one who takes after me the most. What's understood doesn't need to be explained, baby. I Love You! Derek – My Roadie. We didn't come out the same oven, but we're baked from the same batter. Basically, my brother from another Mother. O.V. –

Drag Master Flash, too much to talk about; you already know the vibes bro. My "Sister" FACE, Crystal Renee Hayslett – your training wheels are off now baby and you're pedaling fast; I'm proud of you.

To my son's mother, Tonica, my ex-wife, for giving me my son and showing me that co-parenting never has to be a struggle if both parties want to be respectful, responsible parents. Thank You!

To my daughter, Audriana, who helped me and gave me reason to go above and beyond to be a responsible father.

To my son, Eric, the walking example and reflection of me displaying my never-ending efforts of being the best Father that I can be.

And to Alexus. Although not biologically, you're still my daughter at heart.

To my man AR Muzic – in one word … SOLID! Always been 2 and 10 with it; thank you Bro!

To my road dawg "M". I could write a book on you alone. But in short, I appreciate the whole 29 years and counting homie. You've been the same way. The whole way.

To Str8 A – Ay Chali, my run in Miami would never be what it is if I didn't do what I've done with you; my very first friend in the whole town. Thanks Playa.

To my nieces Imani, Summer, Brooke, Aliyah, Sanai, Mikhalia and Jordie. My nephews Kaleb, David, Allen and Khalil. To my grandchildren Avyanna, Ajiya and Jeremiah. And to the rest of my family – all the Lowe's, Lockette's, Hamilton's, Lewis', Shanks' and Appling's.

Special thanks to Emory "Vegas" Jones, Michael "Chop" Baez and FLO-Rida for the initial encouragement to pursue my mission.

Last, but not least, to my man Jarret Jack, Li Gotti, Free Money Dame, Connie McKendrick and Floyd Mayweather – I'll never forget what all of you have done for me!!

Thank You All!

Preface

The first time I ever attempted to write a book was in the East Jersey State Prison system. Somewhere between '98 and '99. I obviously needed something to do to pass the time. But apparently other things found their way into my thoughts to distract me, because the book is coming into fruition about twenty years later. Guess things really do happen when they're supposed to. And as I think about it, these last twenty plus years were very necessary to ensure a complete story would be written.

And oh, what a story it is. After a checkered life in the streets, social circuits, relationships, and the music industry. Coupled with creating a brand name on social media. I decided it made sense to deliver the background story on how I, and my life became worthy of interest to a culture that has become fixated on the reality of people's lives they encounter and embrace.

Always and forever (for as long as I can remember), I've been the "wear it all on your sleeve" type. Never been good at hiding who I am. Or concealing my emotions. The latter of the two is something I eventually had to conquer. Because my life has been a long deep swim with sharks. And I had to learn to stop bleeding on the outside.

This transcript is a movie in words. A mental vision. You'll see it as you read it. You'll feel it as the ink leaves the paper and writes notes from my life next to reflecting parts of yours. You'll understand that we REALLY ARE one in the same. I'm my people. My people are me. And if you've ever lived anything similar to how I have or damn near identical, then you'll know how essential and integral it is to take self-inventory and *FLIP YA LIFE.*

Introduction

1973, when I was 5 years old, or maybe 1975 when I was 7, I remember my mother telling me, "you're so hardheaded, you're going to learn everything the hard way." No words from my mother have ever rang truer than those.

It was as if no matter what was said to me or by whom, it could be the right or obedient thing to do, but in order for it to result in compliance it needed to personally make sense to me or else I would find a way to alter the instruction to tailor fit my agenda. Now as an adult, with hindsight being 20/20, I've grown to understand, that wasn't the proper way to conduct myself. But I was young. And I needed to figure that out from experience. Which at most times resulted in me getting into trouble. I never concluded that I was doing anything wrong. I was just being myself.

We lived in a bi-level apartment on 34th and Powelton in an area known as "The Bottom". Some say it's called that because of the living conditions and the people were so bad, that it was equivalent to being at the bottom of the barrel. Others say it's simply because any street numbers rather below 40th reflects being at the bottom of West Philly. I wouldn't be surprised if there were older natives with a completely different perspective.

One of my favorite things to do while being hard-headed (as my mom would tell me to stay in front of the building and I didn't) was to disappear across the street from our apartment and into the common area of Kelly Hall at Drexel University. The college students and I alike found one another to be very interesting.

Them, because they were all bigger than me, mostly white, and still made time to engage in conversation with me. And me, because I was this little tiny, intelligent black kid who could hold a full conversation with them. All the while dressed in full cowboy gear; hat, pants and a holster with a gun hanging from each hip. I guess they viewed me as a junior deputy with college potential. That would either grow up to protect the community. Or rival their younger siblings and or children academically. Either way, I was making my presence felt. The fact that I was even there with them confirms how my inquisitiveness overrode direct instruction given to me by my mom. Unknowingly, I was adapting to the habit of challenging or refusing authority to be governed over me. Because the world and everything in it as I see it now and apparently then, is encompassed with rules and regulations that are fixated and imposed by those in positions of power who manipulate others and create benefits for themselves and their immediate circuits.

So, throughout my journey of living and doing things based on the way I perceived they should be done, I collected a lot of life's hard lessons. Those lessons ultimately became my blessings.

Chapter One
Momma's Baby, Daddy's Maybe

Man, I don't know where life starts for me. Maybe it was standing on the corner of my block in West Philly, holding my head because I just finished hitting myself with the handlebars when I was about to get on my bike. Or maybe I've seen the actual picture my mother took that day so many times that it seems like I remember it happening; I was five years old.

The only recollection of life prior to that is another picture of me at 18 months opening an Easter basket where my mom wrote on one picture, "Open it Eric." And on the other picture, I'm holding up the Easter bunny that was in the package, and on that picture my mom wrote "I did it". I was my mom's first born and her heart. And she's mine. She had me at 18 years old. April 19, 1968 at 3:45 pm. In her bedroom, in "Brick City". The name of the projects in Cordele, Georgia; where she lived with her siblings and my grandmother. I was born on a Friday and delivered by a mid-wife. In apartment 508 F.

Being my mom's first born and her being so young, naturally made us close. So much so, that she told me about the time her and my dad got into a fight and he was choking her. Barely able to talk, I intervened saying, "let go my mommy choke." Guess I wasn't aware of the term neck. I wasn't even two years old yet. Turns out that wouldn't be the only time in life I'd run interference when physical harm found my mother. But those details are later in this story.

Before living on the second floor of the bi-level apartment, my mom and I lived on the first floor with my Aunt Ellen, her kids, and her boyfriend. His name was Winky. He used to have this extremely ugly rubber mask he would put on to scare us when we were bad. He called it "Uncle Mike." Yours truly was scared to death of that thing. We lived with them until my cousin Karima and I burned down the entire back room of the apartment playing with matches. That's when my mom and I moved upstairs to a much smaller apartment. And my aunt and cousins had to move to the projects on 56th and Race. I'm not sure if my mom killed me and my life is a resurrection. Or if she knew she'd kill me if she touched me and just didn't. Not long after that my mother's best friend Edna moved from Georgia to Philly to live with us.

We then moved to 33rd and Powelton into an apartment above a dry-cleaning business. The only memories I have from there are the boys I was friends with down the street, and their sister Keisha, and that our kitchen window faced the backyard of Philly's notorious liberation group called MOVE, founded by John Africa. I was a kid, so I didn't understand their purpose until I got older. But I was old enough to know that at any given moment, I could look out that window and see TITTIES. Cause the women walked topless, and freely around their property. Imagine how many times I got caught at that window. Cause it didn't take my mom or Edna very long to figure out what the hell I was up to. That apartment was also the first time I heard the Ojay's "Love Train." I'll never forget that. Essentially it was the start of me loving what we call today "feel good music."

Remember back to me being in Kelly Hall with the students. The part I left out is how I almost gave my mother a heart attack that day. She was inside getting ready for work as a bartender at the Liberty Belle. I was supposed to be in front of the building. Of course, I was not. So, my mom freaked out and called the cops when she couldn't find me. As I emerged from my scholastic gathering with my new upperclassmen friends, I was amazed at the police cars and fire engines parked on the corner. Me, Mr. Inquisitive, walked right up to one of the firemen. And before I could say anything, he said "Is your name Eric?" My silly ass all excited, and smiling, beamed a cheesy "YES!". And on the radio, he said, "I found him." I thought he was a genius to know my name. I had no idea until later in life my mom gave them my description all the way down to the guns.

So, they knew who I was on site. I'd be lying if I said I remember what my mother did to me for scaring her like that. Nevertheless, I certainly figured out that the cops and firemen weren't there to sign me up for either position. Looking back on things, I must say I was bad as hell. And really had it fixated in my mind that I was going to do whatever I wanted to.

One day after coming home from "Get Set," which is the pre-kindergarten program I attended, I proceeded with my normal routine of dressing in my cowboy attire. Only to find my wardrobe was not in its usual place. I asked my mother to share her insight on its whereabouts. You can imagine the look of complete bewilderment on my face when she stated, "All of that stuff is in the trash." In my mind, I'm sure I was thinking I've done things in the past, but not today. Today I was good at school and didn't have any incidents. So, where the fuck was my uniform, especially my guns?! I asked why was it in the trash, and the answer I received was, in my opinion, strange and quite mysterious. "Jehovah doesn't like guns," she said. Now, at the time, I had zero idea what, or who, a Jehovah was. But he, or it, wasn't coming in between me and my appointment with that outfit and my pistols. So, I went right to the trashcan to retrieve my merchandise. That reaction did not sit well with she who dispensed said items to the receptacle. And they once again were confiscated and discarded.

Obviously pissed off at there being no logical explanation; I eventually was made aware of who Jehovah was, once my mother decided we were going to be his witnesses. I wasn't feeling the sudden

14

changes of bible studies, or the new people infiltrating my life with my mother.

I had grown accustomed to the card games, the weed smoke and noticing the little yellow envelopes in which the weed was packaged, signifying that the sweet, familiar aroma would soon fill the air. Part of my leisure on card game night was to sit next to the table where my mom and her friends played Bid Whist. Blasting all the classics from the Jackson 5, Spinners, Stylistics, and all the other greats from that era. Especially the Sound of Philadelphia. Even though it was all adults, my mom didn't kick me out of the kitchen where they congregated. So, in an effort to respect my tender ears and presence, they'd spell most of their curse words instead of saying them. Not knowing I was already good at putting letters together and sounding them out. So, in my head, shit, I was cussin' too.

Life as I knew it at that age consisted of my mom, Edna, their friends, my Aunt Ellen and her kids. My aunt Lillian and my cousin Sheila. But then my mom got a boyfriend. And things got a little tricky.

See my mom was very good friends with my father's siblings. They all grew up in the same town in Georgia and went to school together. So even after my parents weren't involved, my mother was still treated like an extended sister. Which ultimately led my Aunt Ellen to hook my mom up with her boyfriend's brother. He was in Gratersford State Penitentiary in Pennsylvania when they were introduced. When he came home, he landed in our lives. I was around 4 or 5. My only early memories of him and my mom were of them arguing. Which was pretty customary. But the biggest fight I remember is when he came and kicked in the door looking for us and found us cowering between the bed and the wall. When it popped off, I was in the middle, defending my mom and a busted lip was the result. Nevertheless, my mom still let me take school pictures the next day, swollen lip and all. And she wanted to trade in all of this excitement for Jehovah?! I just couldn't understand it.

I was having a hard time adjusting to someone else being in my mom's life. I became very rebellious. It's a wonder I wasn't diagnosed as a child sociopath after burning up the house. Along with the atrocity I'm about to explain next. I was the only child at the time. So, my mom bought me two hamsters. Equipped with the spinning wheels, and tunnels for them to run through and play in. One day (I don't know what came over me) I was playing with one of the hamsters by pushing down on it with the spinning wheel. From there, playing quickly escalated to me beating the hamster 'til he died. My mom almost killed me for doing that. And she made me give the living one to my class.

Of course, there was nothing I could do and was mad. Then not long after that, I remember standing outside of Woolworth's Department store on Market street with my mom and a pigeon shit on her. I don't recall if I laughed out loud. But I damn sure felt good on the inside. I guess I thought it was her payback.

A little while after that, my mom and her boyfriend decided to get married. And the wedding took place in my Aunt Ellen's living room. Can you believe it? The same dude that we had to jump was officially becoming my stepfather. Since I was accustomed to being with my mom so much, you can imagine my surprise and dismay when I heard about something called a "Honeymoon" that required my mom's presence without my approval or attendance. I cried like an infant when they told me I wasn't going. And in an effort to soothe my anguish, my aunt and my cousins recorded themselves singing "Knocks Me Off My Feet" by Stevie Wonder. As part of the song lyrics stated, my aunt assured me that they didn't want to bore me. And that I would be okay. Eventually I was back to normal.

As time went on obviously my mom returned, and life started with her and her new husband David. We moved into one of his brothers, Tom's, properties on Spring Garden Street in West Philly.

17

Of course, I wasn't crazy about moving or about him. And over the ensuing years, I felt the feeling to be mutual. There was just never a bonding period between us. I only remember being chastised by him. I have no fond memories of good times with him. If there were, they just don't stand out to me. So, in fairness I won't say it never happened. But not frequent enough for me to recall anything monumental. But surprisingly one day after I was grown, I pulled up to my mom's house, he was outside and approached me. He congratulated me on the young man I had become. And said that despite no real assistance from him, my biological father, or the poor choices I made that landed me in trouble, he was proud of me and that I should keep up the good work. I can't lie, it felt good. That's actually my best memory of him. So, I can honestly say that I felt horrible when I had to call my brother Kevin years later to tell him his dad had died.

In addition to not liking my stepfather, I hated this new religion. Because it was really cramping my style and how I was used to life operating. Then my mom had the audacity to use her parental powers against me and make me help her pronounce names in the Bible like Nebuchadnezzar, because I was good at reading. I was still six. Then, as if all the current excitement and change in protocol wasn't enough, my mom added more mix to the batter by having a baby. September 8, 1974, my little brother Kevin was born.

I was a great helper to my mom, and I loved my cute little brother, but it was all too clear that my mother's attention was no longer all mine. I guess at the time I didn't know I was jealous but looking back on all the things I did when he was a baby and toddler, it's now apparent that I was.

Still, I remember changing his diapers. Real cloth diapers with the pins, not the fancy Pampers. I was also going to the laundromat to wash those diapers and all the other clothes in the household. Little did I know at the time I was being groomed for the responsibility of adulthood.

Despite my love for my new brother, I still came up with ways to capture my mother's attention. Unconventional ways that almost got me killed at times, but I captured her attention all the same.

Starting with pissing in the bed. Yep, "I'll just lay here and piss in the bed and she'll have to clean the sheets." The truth is I was scared of the dark. So, I was always afraid to get up. Cause my mom left no lights on. That wasn't happening. Or the time I wrote on top of the toilet seat "two kids on a rock, me and Kia, on her cock." And covered it with the seat cover. You know the ones with matching rug and bowl cover? Yeah, that one! Well, me the dummy didn't know that you remove that cover to wash it. So, one day while doing the laundry my mother uncovered my first love song about Kia.

Now notice I said, "my first love song". But that wasn't my first crush. My first crush was my mom's girlfriend, Edna. Very pretty chocolate woman with pearly white teeth and neatly polished red toes. I was around five and developing an appreciation for pretty feet. And then came my first-grade teacher, Ms. Matt. Liking her was inevitable because I had to see her every day. And finally, there was Kia. My 3rd grade crush. By then I was eight years old. And officially titled "mannish". As I stated, I was doing quite a few rebellious things to capture my mom's attention. And the results were consistently almost fatal for me. One day she left me home alone while she visited her friend across the street from where we lived; with the instruction for me to finish my dinner. Well, I absolutely hated mixed vegetables. And there was no way I was going to eat them if I could create an alternative way to get rid of them. My genius mind said, "scrape them out the window." The third-floor window mind you. So, I listened to myself and did exactly that. Not knowing all the while my mother was watching me from across the street from where she's sitting. After her girlfriend said, "Ros, is that Eric throwing food out the window?" My dumb ass was leaning out the window with her groceries sliding off my plate making it rain green beans, carrots and corn. My mom continued her visit. She gave me enough time to think my deceitful venture was successful. Later she came in the house, called me to her presence, told me what she saw, grabbed me by the neck, bent me over with my head locked between her knees, and almost beat the melanin off my ass. 'Til this day I wonder where she came up with that wrestling move.

After almost losing my life over some vegetables, you'd think I learned a lesson about being slick and sneaky. Nah, nope! Not 'cha boy! I actually graduated to being a thief. And FOR SURE could've died this time. My mom was pregnant with my brother Kirby during the fiasco I'm about to explain next. I was attending Alan Locke Elementary School on 46th Street in West Philly. Right next door to the projects. One day I decided to steal a whole TWENTY DOLLARS out of my mom's purse. Not loose change or two dollars. TWENTY!!! And I stopped at Mr. Howard's store on the way to school. My mom always sent me to that store. And NEVER, EVER had it been with a twenty.

So of course, immediately Mr. Howard asked, "Where'd you get this money?" Of course, me, the crook apprentice in training, lied and said, "My mother". He didn't believe me. But still sold me the junk food I wanted and gave me the change. Which I ever so generously distributed amongst my friends by giving them each a dollar. They didn't know I had just hijacked my own mother and made them cohorts in a theft conspiracy. My mom discovered her money was missing not long after I was at school. She knew there were two stores on my route to school. Mr. Howard being the closest to home. So of course, she hit her number on the first roll. He confirmed my purchase with the twenty, and to my third-grade classroom she went.

Super pregnant, my mom came right in that classroom and gripped my crooked ass up and wanted her change. I told her I gave all those kids a dollar and she went crazy. "Whoever he gave a dollar to … GIMME MY MONEY!" she exclaimed through tight lips and clenched teeth. I promise you she retrieved every single dollar. And I think she actually let David whoop my ass for that one. And she called to Georgia and told my grandmother. It was 1976 and my goofy ass was throwing away food and stealing what was considered a fortune in our house at the time. I know my mom had to have been asking herself, "what's wrong wit' this lil nigga?" I was just so hardheaded and inquisitive beyond my own comprehension. My mom was in the back area of our apartment one day and I was in the kitchen. I was supposed to be eating my dinner.

Liver was on the menu. I hated liver. So, behind the refrigerator it went. With any other food I didn't like. I know you're thinking to yourself reading this and saying, "didn't you almost die throwing food out the window fool?" But that was me. Always thinking I was slick and smarter than the whole existence of mankind.

And I would leave the food behind the refrigerator long enough to clean it up once I thought it was safe to do so. I upgraded my disposal system after the mixed vegetables scandal. After I ate, I was supposed to sweep the floor. So, I did. My mom had the stove on because she was about to straighten her hair, but she hadn't come into the kitchen yet to put the straightening comb on the fire. We had a gas stove. As I'm sweeping the floor with that thick handled straw broom, those flames kept whispering to me. "E-riiic. E-riiic. Come play with us!" So, I decided to play swing the broom over the fire. First it was a quick brush over the flame. Then slower, slower, and slower. 'Til the shit caught fire. Exactly as I wanted it to all along. Once it started burning, I put the broom in the sink and ran water on it to put the flame out. My mom smells it. "Eric, what's burning?" "Huh?" I replied as I'm thinking of a master lie. "I said what's burning?" "Nothing." Then I heard feet slam to the floor and start their approach towards the kitchen.

My ignorant ass panicked and started sweeping the floor with the wet, BURNT broom. Water all over the floor. My mom saw that shit and y'all know what happened next. Same wrestling move as with the vegetables. She got busy. And my life is a testament that through all that I STILL never learned or listened.

I was driving my mom crazy. She was about to have a new baby. And things weren't the greatest financially with her new husband. His brother evicted us, and we moved back to Cordele, Georgia where my mom and I originated from.

It was different leaving the city and transitioning to life in the country. Although I was born in Cordele, I didn't know what it was like to live there. Exchanging buses and trains, for walking and dirt roads. And leaving my cousins behind for relatives I didn't really know yet. The first school I attended was Blackshear Trail. Where I had to complete the remainder of 3rd grade. I made friends with this red-head freckle faced white boy named James. James was my buddy, my first experience with a crazy white boy. We would ride the swings together and pretend we were airplanes like in the popular TV show back then, "Ba Ba Black Sheep". The objective was to go as high as possible in the swing to feel like you were actually flying. Then one day, in true crazy white boy tradition, James decided to leap out of the swing in mid to upper air, landing in the grass and dirt; breaking his arm. I thought he lost his fuckin' mind. Although as a kid, he did talk like he was drunk. So, I was done with James and the swings. Still my guy. But it was all ground activities from there on.

My next friend after James was black. His name was Rodney. And he lived two houses over from me. His mom's name was Miss

Mary. But the adults called her "Sugar Foot". I've never in my life heard an adult cuss at kids the way she cussed at us. Rodney and his brothers were accustomed to it. But to me it was foreign because my mom didn't talk like that. But being at their house was still ok with me. Rodney wasn't crazy like James. He was normal. And like me, he loved to play football. And you couldn't tell me I wasn't in the NFL after my dad bought me a Franco Harris Pittsburgh Steeler jersey.

Being back in Cordele was a different life. And besides my brothers Kevin and Kirby, my only other sibling was my brother Scott on my dad's side. My dad was a real piece of work. I was born April 19, 1968. And my brother Scott came right after me six days later on the 25th. Two women pregnant at the same time. Scott was his mother's only child, and he was spoiled, disrespectful, and bad as hell. Way worse than me. Cause he did shit I wouldn't dream of. Like talk back to his grandparents and great grandparents who were raising him.

He didn't like my mom, cause if she said I couldn't come outside then that's what the hell she meant. This nigga would ask her a bunch of damn questions about why. I'm like, "Nigga, will you go back across the street to your great grandmother's house wit' that shit fo you get me kilt". He was so mad at my mom for not allowing me to come outside once, that this fool poked a hole in MY bike tire. Now how the hell was that supposed to hurt her? Dummy! I still ran away from home with him one night on our bikes. With a box of Cookie Crisp cereal as our survival meal. Attempting to ride from Cordele to Atlanta to live with our father. We made it as far as the tip of Interstate 75 and 16th Ave to a Holiday Inn. Where Scott decided to jump in the pool. And then we went home. He didn't get in trouble. I don't know what the hell my mom did to me. But clearly choosing to follow his plan failed.

I had plenty of other relatives in Cordele as well. Primarily my Grandmother, my Aunt Lisa, Aunt Robin, and my Uncles Marvin, Gary and Flint.

My great Uncle Dan Lowe, who was my mom's uncle, and my Uncle Capers, my mom's brother, is where I truly think I developed my swag. Those two dudes were some cool mothafukkaz. My Uncle Capers is still living. And still cool. I remember the clothes and hats they wore. And the cars they drove. Looking back, I can honestly say they were the original definitions of being "Country Boy Clean" in my eyes. But it was my Uncle Flint who used to love to make me come out to the bus stop and show me off to his friends because I could read so well; I was in the 3rd or 4th grade. During this time, I had to get up even earlier than usual for school because he wanted them to know how smart I was.

In my smart-ass mind, I was probably thinking "Why the hell do you have me on this corner basically teaching high schoolers how to read and spell?!" But the truth is most likely I liked the attention and didn't mind at all. The focus was on me. Which was never a hardship for me growing up.

This was the time in my life where I was practically living with my grandmother and songs like "Young Hearts Run Free" and "Heaven Must Be Missing an Angel" were household favorites of my mom's baby sister, my Aunt Lisa. My memories of my mother's favorite groups were The Spinners and Gladys Knight, just to name a couple. A few years go by, I'm now in the 7th grade and my mother was ready to move back to Philly. I, of course, didn't want to move back to Philadelphia. We had been in Georgia for four years and I had grown accustomed to being with my Grandmother and the rest of my extended family. I was starting to recognize and pursue the girls that I liked. And I had established a few solid friendships with guys who I didn't want to depart from. I was fully acclimated to being in the south. And no attachments to anything up North that I was in a hurry to get back to. I mean I had my cousins there. But the sick feeling I had at the thought of leaving Cordele didn't exist when we left Philly. Therefore, it's safe to say, Georgia had my heart. At the moment.

When it was time to move, my mom surprised me by asking if I wanted to stay with "Mudear". Which is what we called my grandmother. It translates to "Mother Dear" in its entirety. Of course, I said, "Yes!" Probably was thinking more like, "Hell Fuck Yeah!" My grandmother had me spoiled and being with her was going to be a cakewalk. Of course, until I managed to fuck it all up.

At the time I was twelve years old. But I actively started trying to get some "action" at age nine. My Aunt Ellen worked at Drexel University. So, one day while I was at a party at Drexel's rec center in West Philly with my cousin Mona. I was dancing and grinding all on this girl. To Taste of Honey's *"Boogie Oogie Oogie."* I remember the massive, unforgettable hard on I experienced that day. I was well aware and aligned with my hormones and sexual desires. So, as I was practically set to be left behind in Georgia, and my mother go off to Philly, what do I do? I get caught getting head from my mother's girlfriend's daughter in the bathroom. My mother didn't catch me. Nor did her girlfriend. The girl's nosey little sister was peeking through the keyhole in the bathroom door. Not knowing precisely what she was witnessing, she went to her mom and best described what she THOUGHT she saw. And that was, I was peeing in her sister's mouth. My mom flipped. By this time, I was about seven or eight years into being a Jehovah's Witness. And the custom in that religion is to go before a board of men known as "The Elders," when you're in trouble for doing things the religion didn't approve of. So, I had to sit and talk to them about why I was gettin' fellatio. I mean they were grown ass men married with children. So, as I think back, questioning me about why I did it was redundant and rhetorical at the very least. And naturally the end result was my mom completely changing her mind and making me move to Philly. That was the first, but not the last time my dick would get me in trouble.

I was on the verge of turning 13 in 1981 and we just moved back to Philly. My mom, her husband David, my brothers Kevin and Kirby, my sister Kim, and myself. Ultimately my mother had six children altogether. My sisters Erica and Elesha being born respectively in '84 and '86.

We were all created incomplete. Because we were meant to be projects requiring consistent effort to evolve from our original state.

Chapter Two
A Change Gon' Come

March 30, 1981 is the day America's most infamous drug trafficker, Ronald Reagan, was shot. He didn't die of course. But the response surrounding the attempted assassination of a President was an obvious big deal. And the first memorable moment after we moved back.

We hadn't been in Philly long. And the transition from country life back to the city was initially uncomfortable. Everything was fast, loud, dangerous and dirty. There was a very intense mob war plaguing the city that started with the murder of Angelo Bruno in March of 1980. And continued as far as I could remember until 1984 with the killing of Salvatore Testa. With more killings in the years to follow. Then there were the neighborhood gangs that were terrorizing the city as well. We lived on the corner of 50th and Woodland in Southwest Philly. And gang activity was very prevalent there. As well as other areas in Southwest known as The Zip and The Bucket. I was young, but still remember guys like Shorty, Tippy and Hungry Jack who were notorious for their street affiliations and fighting.

Although I had lived in Philly before, I was completely clueless to this type of lifestyle or surroundings. I was essentially a country boy implanted into the concrete jungle. The school I had to enroll into was William T. Tilden Middle School on 66th and Elmwood. Where I finished the remainder of 7th grade and all of the 8th. The school was pretty much gang central because it sat in an area conducive to all the surrounding neighborhoods. So, depending on where you were from or if you weren't known, you were definitely a target to get beat up and robbed for your sneakers, jackets, or the popular Space Invader hats. And for sure if you wore jewelry. Sometimes you got jumped for fun. I only got jumped once during my year and a half school term.

Although a couple of my classmates were really cool, popular and liked me, I really didn't have any real protection. One of their names was Butch, he gave me the nickname "Virginia" because of my country accent. The others were Jay, John and Jeffrey. But our interaction didn't exceed being at school because the only friends I could have besides my cousins were those who went to the Kingdom Hall. I found out early on that not everyone who went to the Kingdom Hall were good guys. The ones I knew only went because their mom, or parents made them go. Just like my mom made me.

The seventh grade proved to be monumental for me. Living the city life and finding everything out the hard way. One day I was going to the store on my own and my stepfather told me, "If anyone asks you what gang you're in, tell them you're not in one." I don't recall being asked that question or approached that day. But besides the one time I got jumped on my way home from school, the only other incident I had was getting sucker punched by one of the toughest guys on my block. His name was "Preach." He's dead now. And as I think about it; anyone who has ever harmed me is dead.

I guess it's safe to say I was being bullied for being the new kid on the block and with no neighborhood ties to anyone who would take up for me. So, my beginning stages in Philly were rocky like Balboa. I didn't even have a girlfriend who might have a big brother who liked me enough to not let anything happen to me. I was just fucked. And there were a lot of pretty girls in my neighborhood. But despite my overzealous desire to have a girlfriend, the whole Jehovah's Witness drag was standing firmly in my way. I couldn't even associate with anyone closely outside of family who wasn't a Witness. It seemed as if my life was dictated by everyone except me.

So needless to say, I was pretty miserable at times and felt trapped quite often. My favorite escape from the neighborhood, the Kingdom Hall and my mothers' rules was being at one of three places. My Aunt Lillian's house, or my Aunt Ellen's house (who was also a Jehovah's Witness, but she wasn't as active or strict as my mom). But my ultimate desire was to always be at my Uncle Pierce's house with my Aunt Polly and cousin Gina. It was like being the Fresh Prince of

Mt. Airy when I was there (Mt. Airy is an upper echelon area of Philly).

At my house you'd come close to death if you touched ANY FOOD besides peanut butter and jelly without permission. Everything needed my mother's approval if it was something to eat or drink. Can't tell you how many times I got in trouble for drinking juice and adding water to replace what I drank. I think what pissed my mom off the most about the things I did was the shit that insulted her intelligence. As if she can't taste watered down fruit punch or grape juice.

But at my Uncle's house it was different. They had a couple bucks. At least in my eyes. So, I could eat what I wanted. I always had breakfast, lunch and dinner. And I could even make Steak Umm's without permission. I hated going home after being there. My cousin Gina is partly to blame for me falling in love with gangsta' shit. Cause she's the one who took me to see Scarface when I was 13. And it was over from there.

It wasn't long before it was time to transition to 9th grade and High School. I was accepted into the Communications Magnet at William Penn High School in North Philly, and officially on my way to the next phase of life. I was leaving behind old challenges. And moving forward towards ones where I had no way of knowing what to expect. But still I was excited about the transition regardless of my ignorance to what the future held.

Despite being poor, or not having the latest designer clothes, and wearing thick prescription glasses; I was still very confident, cool, and tried to holla at ANY girl I liked. No matter the outcome. I always just carried this air of confidence about myself, no matter what I didn't have. Sometimes we had no heat or hot water, and we lived on food stamps. But my mom always made it work. And we were clean.

Being in high school was a different experience. I was around new people and it didn't feel as dangerous even though I went to school in North Philadelphia, another rough area. Although I was in the ninth grade, there were Juniors and Seniors who really liked me and always made sure I was good. Especially Ali Khan and Wayne Lassiter (aka Mudd). Both were from North Philly. Ali was the first person I saw with the leather triple fat goose jackets besides Run DMC and Jam Master Jay. But it was Mudd who influenced me to wanna dress fly. He had all the designer jeans, the Top 10 Adidas in all colors, even the patent leather. Crazy waves in his hair and all the chicks.

High school introduced me to more mature and diverse personalities. I was learning how to interact with people on a more educated and intelligent level.

I don't do what men do.

I remove the "n" and I just DO ME.

As you should.

Chapter Three
Can I Live

Fourteen years old in my first year of high school, and still a virgin. Unless you count the "head" I got in Georgia that caused me to be in Philly in the first place. Still, being a virgin sucked because I'd been a little pervert since age five, and still couldn't get no action. But that all changed when I turned seventeen and was in the 11th grade. I finally cracked the code and got my first piece of ass. Life changed and I partially lost my mind.

She was a pretty brown skinned girl from North Philly. I fell all the way into the deepest depths of love. She had me twisted like Keith Sweat stuck on a trigonometry equation. Everything about this girl had me open like the welfare office on the 1st and 15th. From the way she smelled, to the shape of her body. I'm telling you; I caught a bad one! Even with the glasses. Iz you shittin' me?! And I had no problem expressing my feelings and infatuation in front of the entire school. One of the times my father sent me some money, I used some or all of it to buy her some navy blue and white Cortez Nike's. I brought the sneakers to school and gave them to her in the lunchroom at the table with all her girlfriends there. And didn't give a damn about who laughed at me. Cause there was plenty of jokes about me being all caught up. But I didn't care. 'Cause all I was thinking 'bout was the next early dismissal, or hooky day with Eric and Jon or Chuck so we could get our chicks and fornicate like the hell bound sinners we were.

Having a girlfriend did give me a different type of confidence. Especially when it came to dealing with guys who liked to clown and play a lot. There was one particular person who had developed a bad habit of thinking shit was sweet. I can't front. He was a fly nigga from South Philly. He had that silky wavy shit on his head. He was also the first person I knew to drink syrup. Known today as "lean". One day he was fuckin' with me and I'd had enough. I was tired of this nigga. And to the pleasure of most people, I whooped his ass. Until my friend Jon stepped in and stopped it. And I wasn't even a tough guy. But everyone has their limits. And I had reached mine with him. So, we handled business. And continued being classmates afterwards. We even spoke years later and interacted at one of our graduating class functions.

It wasn't long after I had a girlfriend, that I didn't have a girlfriend anymore. Not only was she a year older than me. But she was also a cheerleader. And a basketball player is who I lost her to. So, in an effort to mask the hurt, I concentrated more on the rap group I had started with my two friends, Eric "DJ Prep" Daye and Jon "Jon Doe" Hamilton. We were the Devastating Three and very popular

38

around the school. I wasn't a "fly guy," but I could rap my ass off. And that's what added to my cool.

Nevertheless, I was still living under these Jehovah's Witness rules and I still wasn't allowed to go to parties. Then one day I decided I wasn't going to listen to my mom, again, and I went to a party on a Saturday night after I got off work from my job at Larry's Steaks and Hoagies. I was 17 and I was starting to buy better clothes because I had a job. So, after a bus, train, subway and trolley ride from West Philly to North Philly, I was on my way to being one of the cool kids for the night. But facing possible death when I got home. I finally made my way to the block where the party was. It was on 6th and Parrish. And as I was approaching the house where the party was being held, I saw the girl who was supposedly my girlfriend coming around the corner. We had gotten back together after the basketball player. Or so I thought. But now here she was with a whole new dude. Wit' her cheatin' ass. Her house was on the same block as the party. And as I was approaching her and the guy, her mother happened to be looking down at us from the window. You know most hood moms back in the day used their bedroom windows as watch towers to give them a view of both ends of the block and as far forward as they could see. So, before anything unnecessary could take place, she called for us to come into the house. "I'm tired of you and this nonsense," her mother said, talking to her daughter. "Which one of these boys is your boyfriend?" And without pause or hesitation, she announced the other guy.

Of course, I was devastated. Along with the fact that I was definitely going to be in trouble when I got home. The trolley and subway ride home were about to be long and dreadful.

The next day was Sunday; long, awful, stomach hurting type of day. Monday, back to school and now I must face her. I don't know how many love letters I wrote over the weekend, but it didn't matter. She was gone, with no intention of coming back. I was so hurt and angry, I ended up punching a window in school and had to get stitches in my fist; I still have the scars to this day. For the first time in my life, I was learning about having your heart broken.

Being seventeen and a Jehovah's Witness was conflicting more by the day. I was becoming frustrated and increasingly rebellious. All the things that came to me naturally as a human that I didn't even have to apply myself to, were being denied due to this religion. I was a natural born athlete. But I wasn't allowed to play sports. Loved women all my life. And came from a bloodline of male whores. But wasn't supposed to have a girlfriend. I felt like a Boa Constrictor was wrapped around my life. Ever since I was a kid my mom always drilled in me to "keep a low profile." And she wanted me to wear argyle sweaters and penny loafers. But that wasn't me. I'm a high-profile guy. It got me where I am today. I learned when and how to turn the profile down. As necessary. But my collective of talents and desires were fighting to be satisfied.

Eric, Jon and I entered the school's talent show, I knew we would kill it. Rapping was where I carried the most swag and confidence. I knew I was nice. One of the judges for the show was Wendy "Lady B" Clark. She was a well-known on-air radio personality in Philly on Power 99 FM. And also, the first female artist to actually record a rap song for a record. It was called "To The Beat Y'all". After the show she autographed my sweatshirt and I got airbrush over her signature so the ink from the pen would never fade her name.

Yeah, I was a fan! And I was crushing on her too! Lookin' and smellin' like a hundred million to my young horny nose. She wore Calvin Klein's Obsession perfume and a full-length mink dragging the floor. Like a Mississippi Madam with a full stable. So, imagine my excitement when she told me she was looking for an intern and brought me on. I was happy as a crook with a bag of stolen money and a guaranteed escape route. I would go to the radio station every day after school. And then on Sundays she had her Street Beat hip-hop show on air from noon to four. She even had Street Beat MC's. Prince Little E, Disco C and Flash D (The Green-Eyed MC).

The way it worked was every Sunday, about 3:55 she would put on a popular instrumental and let everyone spit their rhymes. ON AIR. So, they were very popular. When I came on board Flash was locked up. And no one knew I could really rap. I don't think "B" remembered me rapping at the talent show. But one Sunday I bust my gun and let Little E hear my rhymes. He immediately told "B" I should rap with them. After that I was known as "Eazy E," the Street Beat MC. The illest shit was the girls who used to call in to the station from all over the tri-state area to speak to their favorite MC. So, when calls came in from females who wanted to speak to me, you couldn't tell me shit. Sunday's became my favorite day of the week.

The more I worked with "B," the less I listened to my mom. And without a doubt … it was a (w)Rap Snack for being a Jehovah's Witness. And surprisingly my mom stopped making me participate. But her new concern was the times I was coming in her house at night. After repeated attempts at talking to me about coming home late. She finally drew the line in the sand and said, "You turn 18 in a few days. The next time you come in my house after midnight, you're gettin' out!"

42

April 19th, 1986, I was with "B" and the whole crew earlier in the day. She gave me a birthday cake. By nightfall I was with my friends and doing who knows what. But whatever it was, it delayed me gettin' my ass home before midnight. Now, if my mom tells this story, she says I came home the next afternoon. Which I don't think my nuts were hanging THAT low, but I do remember coming in after 12 for sure. I went to bed and my mom woke me up out of my sleep saying, "Whoever dropped you off, call them and tell them to come back and pick you up. You thought I was playing?! You're getting out my house!"

Now add the big birthday cake sitting on top of her Jehovah's Witness refrigerator to me coming home late, that just upgraded my disrespect from offensive to egregious. But without hesitation, I called my friend back to pick me up and I was off to forced/voluntary by default independence.

I moved to North Philly with my friend who lived with his dad, uncle and grandmother. There was no heat or hot water, and my "bed" was a loveseat. Since it was April, it was still kind of chilly at night. So, sleeping on that plastic covered chair with my knees constantly bent was cold and uncomfortable.

I either washed up in a pot with warm water from an electric hot plate. Or thugged it out sometimes with a cold shower. My Uncle

Pierce had gotten me a job at his friend's car wash, and me and my friend Chuck delivered pizzas for Dominoes.

Chuck and I had been friends since I moved to Philly. My first real friend from the Kingdom Hall. That lasted for years to come. Our mothers treated us both as if we were their own. His mom, Ms. Carmen, even disciplined me like I was hers. She even almost served me instant death by way of possible diabetes one time. We ate pancakes for breakfast one Sunday. And I put way too much syrup on mine. And just like in my mom's house, wasting food of ANY kind was a capital offense. So even after I had eaten all the pancakes, she also made me eat the syrup by itself. I almost died. And she cared not one bit. Even after I was an adult and reminded her about it, she said, "You shouldn't have poured all that syrup on those pancakes. You know we don't waste food."

That job at Dominoes wasn't the only way I was surviving. My other income came from selling powder cocaine and a little crack at the time. One of my homies from out Southwest who I went to school with, gave me my first pack. After seeing how he dressed and the money he was gettin', I wanted in. So, he put me down and I took it from there. And even after being kicked out the house and figuring out independence, I still managed to graduate High School in June '86 with a high "C" average. And yes, my mother was in attendance.

Putting me out was tough love. She had to choose between letting me stay and defy her rules and drive her crazy or take control of her mental well-being and raise her other five children. I gave her no choice except to choose the latter.

However, she did allow me to come home the following February after being gone 10 months. I was settled into my independent ways and absolutely had no intentions of going back to The Kingdom Hall. When we talk about it these days, she says she wishes she kept making me go, but I'm glad she didn't. It wouldn't have made a difference. Because my mind was already made up that I was going to do what I wanted to do.

While I was living out of the house for 10 months, I caught my first real charge when I was arrested at the King of Prussia Mall for boosting (shoplifting). The case resulted in probation, so I wasn't trippin' too hard. By the time I was living back at home, I was moving with a different type of swag. The glasses had been replaced with contact lenses. And stealing clothes had boosted my appetite to dress better than I had all my life.

Now imagine the irony when I started working with a cleaning crew in Bloomingdales at the King of Prussia Mall by the time, I was 19 or 20. After I had been arrested out there for stealing. We were responsible for cleaning the store before it opened. How convenient it was that no one was around except us. And the machines to take the sensors off the clothes remained on. No security. No cameras. We were KILLIN 'em. And nothing I stole was for sale. It was strictly for wardrobe enhancing. Looking back now I wish I had a different mentality. I would've sold all that shit. Nevertheless, Guess, Bugle Boy, and an abundance of Le Coq Sportif dominated my wardrobe.

Maybe a year and a half to two years after that I hit a real lick when I got a job as a security guard overseeing an entire warehouse of Mickey Mouse clothing, which was extremely popular at the time. There was no way I was going to work around all that inventory ALONE and not take it. I used to have my man come there, back his car up to the main doors and we loaded as much shit in his car as we could. We did this every Sunday until we had every style and size of everything they sold in our possession.

This time I was a lil' smarter than before. I sold more than I kept. And the paper was good. We had damn near the whole West Philly in Mickey Mouse gear. Especially Parkside.

Don't be embarrassed about what you don't know.
Be embarrassed if your pride interferes with you
asking questions to educate yourself.

Chapter Four
From Philly to Brooklyn

In the late 80's, and early 90's is when my friends Wiz, Romeo, Lovie, Pro, Chauncey, Wendell, Tank and Wayne and I started partying a lot in New York. Union Square and Latin Quarters were our primary destinations. Wiz was the best dancer in the crew (Romeo would argue that) and went on to dance for DJ Jazzy Jeff and the Fresh Prince. Unfortunately, he was later killed in a car accident in Jersey.

Being in New York and interacting with people in the music industry added to my developing authentic networking abilities. And while I was getting familiar with the hip-hop culture, I was also learning more about the streets. On one hand I was learning the ropes of how to slide through the clubs knowing who was looking for coke to snort and sell it undetected. And on the other hand, I was simply being recognized as one of the guys from Philly who liked to dance and party. We really started to make a name for ourselves from Philly to New York.

Being with my friends was a big deal to me. Besides the fun we had, it was also as if I finally had my own solid foundation of guys who would be there for me if ever the need occurred. Neither my biological father nor my stepfather was integral in my life. So, a lot of things really got figured out through trial and error. Or in other words, "the hard way". Just like my mother said since I was seven.

In the midst of all the partying we were doing, we met some rappers and dudes who were dancers for rappers. It was a really big deal to have at least some sort of dance moves. And being in a crew only amplified your presence. So, the club scene was our boardroom. And meetings were scheduled regularly. The thing that got us going about dancing, obviously was the music. Stetsasonic, Masters of Ceremonies, UltraMagnetic MC's, just to name a few, were some favorites to dance to. But if you ever wanted to see the team go off, Boogie Down Productions was all you needed to play. KRS-ONE is a master lyricist who commandeered some of the hardest beats of that era. With his DJ Scott La Rock backing him up. Scott was even celebrated on a very popular record, that labeled him a "Super Hoe". *"Scott La Rock had 'em all. He is a Super Hoe."* But we probably really were captivated by them because of their album cover and title; CRIMINAL MINDED. Where they posed with big guns and heavy ammunition. Rappers with the persona of gangsters. It was different. But dope.

So, you can imagine the anguish we felt on August 27th, 1987, when it was reported that Scott La Rock had been killed trying to intervene in a fight. It marks the first time an entertainer I knew of and

49

liked, had lost their life. It was as if a friend died. About three and a half years later, the biggest personal loss of life happened upon us.

Valentine's Day 1991 is one of the worst days ever. My ex-girlfriend's brother, Darryl Huntley, was killed by Terri Harper, a rogue off duty police officer and her then boyfriend, Donnell Drinks. They were looking to rob his home, thinking he was someone else and had assumed the home was a drug stash house, containing large amounts of money. On their quest, they stabbed and tortured Darryl. Also known as Ali Sharine Sadat Shabazz. Which is where I got the idea for my Muslim name.

They also handcuffed and cut the wrists of his girlfriend who was with him. Miraculously she survived. Terri and I were classmates at William Penn High. And as I was reading the newspaper article about what happened, my mind was blown after seeing her name and face. I never knew she had become a cop. And certainly, had no idea she was capable of participating in such a heinous crime.

We were very cordial in high school. And she was a cool chick. Yet she's responsible for that cold, rainy, late night "9-1-1" page I received on my beeper from Sharine's cousin Dul, also known as "Pro" as I slept on the couch at my mother's house. Dul picked me up and we went straight to Hahnemann University Hospital where they had taken Sharine. By the time we arrived, his sisters Trish and Jaycina

50

greeted me and told me he was gone. I asked where he was. They showed me the room and I walked in. There he was. Laying freshly murdered, with blood still dripping from his neck (from them cutting his throat) onto the gurney he laid on. And from the gurney to the floor, and on my Timbs. I stood there in utter disbelief. He was a champion boxer in the Pennsylvania penile system. A mean barber. And a natural comedian. And the WORST rapper in the world (as I sit her reminiscing and laughing my ass off)!

Sharine came from a family of well-dressed hustlers, who knew how to get fly and get into some gangsta shit if and when it was necessary. And for the whole time we ran together, those characteristics were taught to, and rubbed off on me.

Unlike when I started my tenure with my Brooklyn niggaz. What I learned from them was you could be with a dude every day of your life and he'd kill you, go to your funeral, hug your mom and promise to find out who did it. But standby. More about Brooklyn coming up later.

Sharine's other cousin, Mohammad, was my 1st OG. And when I was 21-22 years old, "Mo", as we called him introduced me to the VIP lifestyle. All of us were going to the hottest clubs in Philly. And labeled as "Very Important" in each venue. Whenever we arrived, all things stopped. Managers surfaced to greet us outside or instructed

51

security to ensure our entrance was only delayed by us stopping to speak to those who may have known us as we entered the building. And of course, searching us was out of the question. I mean for what?! What they would have been checking for was certainly right there in its proper place. Sometimes there was already "Shamp" (which is what we called champagne) at the table when we arrived. This was customary in most clubs we frequented.

Mohammad lives by the Jay-Z credo, "If every nigga in yo' clique is rich, yo' clique is rugged. No one would fall 'cause everyone would be each other's crutches." I counted my first hundred thousand with Mo. He epitomized everyone shining and looking good. He didn't like being the only one looking like a boss.

I remember when my ex-wife and mother of my son and I started dating, Mo made sure I represented well on our first date. He gave me his burgundy 560 SEL Benz to drive. At that time, that was the big boy whip. So, when I came through her block on Beechwood Street uptown, with my man behind me, back to back in his Benz, with the systems blaring, it was a real demonstration for her neighbors to see.

Even though Mo was my OG, his cousin Abdul was my day in and day out partner in crime. I met him when I was 18 or 19 at my girlfriend's house. Who as I said earlier was Sharine's youngest sister

52

and Dul's first cousin as well. One day we were all out in front of her house on 10th and Thompson, in the Harrison Projects in North Philly listening to music and dancing. Her mom loved to see me dance. Then someone said, "He can't dance better than Vernon" (which is Pro's government middle name). So, he was called, and he came right over. He only lived across the street. When he arrived, an all-out dance off was in play. It was dope. I actually picked up a few additional moves to add to the "Whop" that day. From that day forward, him and I were inseparable. He's the reason I started partying and going to New York.

It wasn't long before him and I ventured into the streets to get money together. It's not like we were getting paid to dance. So, it was time to transition. In the midst of our street capers, him and I also became a rap duo together. We did a lot of recording, and even came close to a record deal with West Philly native and Original Gangsta rapper Schoolly D. We even travelled and opened for him a few times.

But you know how the story goes when you're playing with fast money. Everything else slows up, takes less precedence, and you delve deeper into the pace of the "game". Until it all unravels, the lights go dim, and the show abruptly stops.

One night, Pro and I were bowling, and his pager went off. He asked me, "Yo! Did Mo just hit you?" And as I was about to say no, my pager went off as well. And it was the dreadful "1-1-9," to signify that something more egregious than a normal 9-1-1 had occurred. Mo actually came up with that emergency code after Sharine got killed. So, we knew if that code ever came through there was no time for games.

Thankfully no one was hurt or dead. But the urgency was that the Feds were doing raids through our entire faculty. From North Philly to West Philly over to South West. And the way we were connected to one another, each time they left one location we were predicting who's house they were going to next. And we continued to be spot on. Pro and I actually pulled up to one of the locations, his cousin Len's store, and we sat from a distance watching those fukkaz. The same way they apparently had been watching us.

After they left, we went inside to talk to his cousin, and he said he heard on the radio that the next location was their other cousin's house. So, as I'm paying attention to the route, it's my guess that South West Philly is coming up soon or next. That's where my mom's house was. So, I called her. My mom doesn't play any police games when it comes to her kids. If the cops were looking for me, she will tell them NOTHING. And she is not opening her door.

But this was different. I got her on the phone and told her, "Mommy, the cops are going to come to your house. When they arrive, let them in. Cause if you don't, they're going to kick in your door."

54

She asked if I had anything in there and I assured her that I did not. All the drugs and guns I used to store under my little brother Kirby's mattress had been removed long ago. Surprisingly and thankfully though, they never showed up. They did go to South West, but it was to one of our other homies' house. Needless to say, that was a stressful ass night.

Pro's house had been hit, so naturally he wasn't going home until we figured out what the fuck was going on. So, for the next few days, we got low and played the hotel in Chinatown until we finally went to see his lawyer, Lou Savino, to get insight on the situation. And sure enough, there was an 18-count indictment on our entire team and some other affiliates whose names I recognized. Sitting in that office and hearing the reality of what was happening felt like the wind was getting knocked out of me.

As I read through the paperwork, I started to notice the craziest shit. There were a few incidents they had under surveillance, with descriptions of Pro's movements that had his name, but they always had "accompanied by an Unknown Male" next to it. Of course, based on the incidents being read, we knew they were referencing me. What was unclear to all of us was, why they didn't name me or ultimately indict me too. I was notorious for getting locked up with guns at the time. And probation was always the outcome. But I escaped that indictment. Some people didn't like it. But the bottom line was, I wasn't going to ask or debate with those people about why they didn't come for me. I took it as a blessing. As any sensible person would.

One night there was a shooting at a club in West Philly. Studio West. And a lot of people got taken in for questioning. This girl we knew happened to be one of them. And she told me later that while she was in the detective's office, she saw a bunch of pictures of all my friends and I on the floor. Unfortunately, that warning was too late. The indictments were already out. And it wasn't long before all my guys, Mo and Pro included, were gone to do their time.

Those damn cell phones caused the demise of everyone. All that thinking you're talking in code shit is a lie. Them people had all that shit broken down to a science with the meaning of everything that was "code" right next to it. For example, "Half a sheet cake" was a half a kilo or 18 ounces of cocaine. But of course, the game hasn't changed. And niggaz are still gettin' money and talkin' on phones. And the Feds are still listening and locking them the fuck up. Except for these new folks who use social media to voluntarily forfeit their freedom by willingly broadcasting their crimes. The cycle of the game continues.

I spoke earlier about my involvement with guys from Brooklyn. And now I'll elaborate on how it all began.

One day while I was working as a salesman in the Gallery Mall at Trends II clothing store, a group of guys came in. They wore camouflage shorts, Timberland boots and bandanas on their heads like Aunt Jemima. One of them really took a liking to me. His name was "G," they called him "Chicken Boy", he was from Brownsville in Brooklyn. They turned out to be some really dangerous guys. And they introduced me to another level of the streets.

I was still working my regular job and had gotten further into the habit of dressing nice and wearing jewelry. My first jewelry set; a nugget watch and bracelet came from my income tax money. But my jewelry was nothing like theirs. They wore big rope chains or the huge Gucci links. Or the popular chains with the Lazarus piece on it. G's signature was his red Jeep Cherokee with the black rag top with 4x4 carved out on each of the rear sides of the truck. Whenever he was coming through, you'd know. Cause you would hear those fifteens knocking from at least two blocks away 'cause he rode with the back hatch lifted. His favorite tunes were En Vogue's *Hold On.* Or Soul II Soul *Back to Life,* acapella. The way those guys moved was nothing like anything I'd ever witnessed. The intrigue caused me to link up with them and start gettin' money. He had a spot on 42nd and Brown that was doing about 10k a day. So, he made room for me to eat.

I'll always remember my first encounter hanging out with them. There was a huge rap show in Philly. About 20 of these guys, 5 cars deep, came to my mother's house to pick me up to go to a concert. Big Daddy Kane, Slick Rick, and a lot of other people were on the show. We were at the back of the building at the ramp that goes down to backstage and I remember they kept saying, "When we see Scoob and Scrap, don't worry about it, they got us, we gonna be good!" And when the van carrying Big Daddy Kane and his dancers came to the ramp, both Scoob and Scrap got out and made sure we were all backstage.

That was my first backstage experience and it was dope; I even took a picture with Slick Rick that day. Posing with the big pinky ring I had just recently bought with "ERIC" in diamonds. After the concert, we were all ready to leave and I have no idea what happened, but a big fight broke out in the parking lot between my guys and some other guys. All I remember is the trunk of the car that I was riding in got popped open and out came what was either a M100, a Mac 10 or 11 or a Tec-9. I'm not 100% sure. Because I don't really remember. But those were the guns of choice back then. So, I'm sure it was at least one of them.

I was having an adrenaline rush of fear and excitement at the same time once those guns came out. All you saw and heard was running and screaming while those bullets were flying. Life on a roller coaster was just beginning.

I was just getting to know these guys as we hung out. I was closest to G. He was so paranoid and trusted no one. And I learned that people who don't trust, can't be trusted. They see in others what's in themselves. Being with him every day brought things out of me that I didn't know existed. Like the time I broke a guy's hand with a hammer for stealing. I definitely had become influenced by my association.

It was weird to see my other man Stink Boogie, who was G's right hand, be so close to him, yet so different. He was an asshole. But he wasn't ruthless. And he was fair. A lot of people got paid because of Stink. G would rather kill 'em than pay 'em. Hire somebody else. And probably kill them eventually.

Stink was a shit starter though. Dudes always got caught slippin' 'cause they never knew when he was being serious or joking. One time we were in a room at a hotel after party and some dudes were arguing. I don't remember the complete dynamics, but one of the guys diverted his attention away from who he was talking to, and looked at me and said, "I'll fuck him up." Stink says, "Oh E (that was my nickname then) you gotta fight him!" So of course, it was on. My shoulder dislocated while fighting. Which placed me at an immediate disadvantage. And Stink, G, and the rest of our niggaz almost killed that boy. Which is what Stink wanted to do all along. Dude saying something to me was the perfect reason to set it off. Stink just made it seem like it was about to be a fair one.

Don't allow prison to be glorified in your eyes. Once you're inside, you never know what could cause you to never be able to leave.

Chapter Five
Get It How You Live

It wasn't much later that G went to jail to do some time on Rikers Island. When he got out, he was supposed to come back to Philly. Unfortunately, he never made it back. I talked to him on a Monday and he was supposed to be on his way. Tuesday, I didn't hear from him. Wednesday morning, I called his mother's house because he wasn't answering his beeper and I asked his mother, "Where is he?" She said, "I don't know, he didn't come in here last night. He's probably over at that girl's house." And as his mother and I were talking, she said, "Hold on," someone was at her door. She came back to the phone and she said, "They killed him!"

I said, "Huh?!"

She said, "They killed him!"

I asked, "They killed who?!"

She said, "They killed Gene!"

I asked again, "Who?"

She said, "I don't know, that was the police at my door, and they showed me a picture of him and he's dead!"

I was standing on the corner of 52nd and Jefferson at the pay phone outside of the deli. Speechless. I got off the phone with his mom and was in a haze of disbelief.

I replayed in my mind all the things that I knew he'd done to people. As well as the things I'd heard. It was then clear to me, that if you lived a certain way that you'll possibly die that way.

When someone shoots you 18 times, they're making sure you don't survive. When I spoke to one of the girls in Philly he dealt with, she told me she was on the phone with him apparently right before it happened. We used to have this thing where we would rate on a scale of 1-10 the level of tension we felt when something didn't feel right. And she said while they were talking, he said he felt tension. She asked him how much. He said a 9. She told him to go in the house and he said he was. But he never made it.

Not long after that Me, Pro, Stink Boogie, and one of G's chicks, Brooke, took that long limo ride from Philly to Brooklyn to pay our last respects. When I viewed his body, I could see where he had been shot in the face. It was sad to see him go out like that.

Despite all his shortcomings, I missed him. And so did my family. My mother still talks about him to this day because she will never forget the time he gave her a television set and a VCR. And my youngest brother Kirby always reaches out to me on the anniversary of his death, May 4, 1992.

Him and my brother Kevin loved Chick to death. He treated them like his little brothers. Chick ran into Kevin one day while Kevin was on his way home from school and took him to buy him some new sneakers. He never forgot that day. Kirby went to school at Dobbins in North Philly. And one day he paged me from the lunchroom pay phone at school. He had gotten into a fight, but the guy said he was going to get my brother jumped after school. I showed up to my brother's school as they were getting out, with Chick and about 12 other niggaz from Brooklyn and Philly. Two Jeeps and two cars deep. Champion hoodies or crew necks, camouflage pants, bandanas and Timberlands were most likely the uniform. It was automatic concern cause Philly niggaz didn't dress like that. Guns in the cars. Knives in our pockets, and razors under the tongues. It was going to go really bad if my lil' brother got touched. But after that presentation, he had no problems. That day or going forward.

Chick had his good ways, but he was a very dangerous guy and I lived life day in and day out with him and people like him.

Kirby told me that any time I wasn't home, he wouldn't go to sleep until I came in the house. No matter what time it was. Even on a school night. Sometimes I came in too late and he would go to school after having no sleep. So, if that's how it affected him, as my little brother, imagine what my mom was going through. These are the things I put my family through because of the choices I was making.

My life has to have purpose!

I've been around too many dangerous situations where I could have lost my life or taken someone else's.

Like the time I chased this guy down Jefferson Street in West Philly with a gun aimed at his back, trying to pull the trigger. But the gun jammed. I still think about how disastrous my life could have been had I shot that man and gone to prison for that. Or the time this dude from Brooklyn had me at gunpoint in a second-floor apartment over some shit Chicken Boy did, but dude thought it was me. You know it's all bad when homie got tears in his eyes telling you that you stole money from him that was meant for his daughter. Not knowing the whole time Chick's paranoid ass had found homies stash and thought HE was stealing. And Chick took the money. In his weird way of thinking, a person couldn't have been saving the money they earned from him and Stink paying them. If Pro wasn't in that room with us, I would have for sure been shot that day.

Change is only bad when you're changing for the worst.

Chapter Six
From the Hammers to the Slammer

It wasn't until the age of 29 that I finally went to prison. And for what? Another gun. Except this time, it wasn't Pennsylvania, it was New Jersey. And once they saw my rap sheet, they had no interest in playing games with me. There was the arrest with the .357 when I was randomly stopped and searched walking across the street down 46th and Walnut. The cops said they saw a bulge under my shirt. Searched me, found the gun, and arrested me. Had that gone to trial, I would have probably beat that charge using the *Terry v Ohio* case reference. Then one day, I was on the corner of 55th and Woodland and the cops pulled up all crazy out of nowhere, so I broke out running. I had a Mac 11 on me with a 32-shot clip. As I was running up Woodland Ave and down Allison Street, I was able to pop the clip out and throw it. My dumb ass should have just thrown the whole fuckin' gun. But my adrenaline was going. And I was overthinking. So, I fucked that all up. And when I turned the corner to go up 56th street, the cops were coming towards me in the car, and another one on foot was behind me. Empty gun in hand, they locked me up. And they didn't even beat me up for running.

Another day I was on the pay phone on Jefferson Street outside of my man Len's store. My back was towards the street. As I turned around, the jump outs were pullin' up on me and I didn't have time to run. I was strapped with a .38 and was stuck. Locked the fuck up AGAIN. All three cases were eventually consolidated to one probation. And I think I was finished with my probation by late '95 after 3 years. But in '96 I got locked up again for aggravated assault with a handgun and kidnapping. But I beat it because the accuser never went to court. So, there was no conviction. But despite that fact, New Jersey would still see it on my jacket, along with all the other guns and probation. So, when Jersey State Troopers arrested me in Camden with a .45 automatic, they didn't hesitate to give me three years in the East Jersey State Prison system. And what pissed me off the most was, I didn't know I was getting sentenced the day that I did. I thought it was just going to be another scheduled court date since most times you come back for sentencing. I didn't have a chance to get my affairs together and have a date to turn myself in. The day that they told me it would be three years is the day that I got sent up state; my son was ten months old.

And just that fast, there would be no more flying up and down 76 in my white Acura Legend, listening to Bad Boy artists, Tupac, or Monifah and AZ zoning out while I'm running the streets.

My son was screaming "Da Da" from the back of the courtroom as I'm standing in front of the Judge. The emptiness I felt that day was unexplainable. Not to mention I was completely ruining my marriage at the time.

Infidelity in my marriage was one of the worst decisions I made as a young man. A good woman shouldn't have to endure that level of pain. Unfortunately, I just didn't know any better and was making the mistakes most people would when they are basically learning about life as they go. Having a man in my life to school me in this area would have been instrumental. But I didn't have that. And because girlfriends weren't allowed in my mother's house growing up, I was never properly prepared for relationship conduct and protocol.

Cheating on your wife is an absolute no-no. Leaving home for another woman is a Hell No! I allowed ignorance to destroy my household. I was living life; having a good time, while making a difference in another woman's life. She wasn't accustomed to wearing designers such as Donna Karan and Coogi dresses and skirts. Or going to parties with celebrities like Mary J. Blige, Total, and drinking Cristal with Allen Iverson. It felt good showing someone things they'd never seen. But what I was blind to, is that it was all being done for someone who didn't deserve or appreciate it.

And while I was trying to teach her about the "lifestyle", I was learning about it myself. Even as it related to fashion. Or just dressing appropriately. When I was younger, being with Mohammed, we

69

dressed a different type of fly when we went out. Suits, ties, alligator or crocodile shoes. Jeff caps or Borselini's. Real gangsta attire. But then came the high-end fashion that consisted of Dolce & Gabbana and Versace. My homies POP and Bryce were the first guys I knew to actually wear Versace after hearing Biggie rap about it. Coogi and Polo was more my budget. But hey, I was still fly and dressed very nice.

Going to prison really changed my life and perception. It also marked when the words of my mother saying I'd learn the hard way because I don't listen, finally manifested. I was sitting in the hole at East Jersey State Prison in Rahway and realized I was finally faced with the results of not adhering to my mother's teachings.

Clothes and a great body make you look nice.

Your character determines if you're attractive.

Chapter Seven
Poor Choices, Worse Results

I'd be lying if I said there weren't more mistakes to come. I wasn't perfect, so of course I made more. Although they were minimal. Because I was finally starting to grasp the importance of listening, comprehending and applying. The overall moral is you'll either listen and learn or hear and ignore. But be assured that despite which of those two apply to you personally, there's a lesson coming regardless.

Another thing I learned and had no choice about accepting in my life was the reality of receiving back what I put out to others. Some call it Karma. In Islam, it's called Kifarah. When I got married, August 5, 1995, it was one of the best, and at the same time, most confusing days of my life.

I had been sitting in the Detention Center on State Road since sometime in June, awaiting the outcome of a shooting I was charged with. I was on probation when I got locked up, so a detainer was holding me until my original sentencing judge decided whether or not to lift it. So, I could be able to post bail.

To my surprise and relief, he eventually did remove the hold, and my bail was paid. It was an interesting two months to say the least. Equipped with a riot in the jail, caused by an officer being knocked out by a Muslin. And them injecting him with Thorazine to get him under control. Once they called religious services on F Dorm that night, the Muslims came out and got right into action with the guards.

Shit was on the news and everything.

When I was finally released, it was the early morning of the day we were getting married. August 5, 1995. Around 2 am. And that could be considered the good part. The confusing/bad part is I was nervous and scared to death about getting married. Because I wasn't sure about what the hell I was doing. But in no way did I have the heart or the balls to call it off. So, within the following 24 hours, I'd become a married, confused man fresh out of the county and on a ship to the Bahamas for our honeymoon.

Three weeks later I did the unthinkable and met another woman. Who I, like an idiot, fell in love with and started an extramarital affair. This was with the undeserving woman I mentioned earlier.

Of course, I could blame the fact that I really didn't have my father or a father figure to explain to me about the detriments of my decisions. But being responsible later made me realize that I was wrong and just never should have allowed anything or anyone to disrupt my marriage. Some of my old friends did speak to me occasionally about it because they knew and liked my wife. But my man Taheem was the hardest on me. Because he's the one who told me EXACTLY how that whole thing would play out. Using Ginger and Ace (the characters from the movie Casino) as his examples of the other woman and myself. He knew I was caught up with someone who was not good for me. Funny how people on the outside see your situation better than you. And you're the one IN IT. Years later my man POP told me, "Nigga, I knew you was fucked up over her when you went to jail and told me to take care of her and not your wife." Not that I didn't care about my wife. I knew she had family support. And I wanted to show the other one I had her back even in my absence. Yeah, I was bugged the fuck out. Or in layman's terms … PUSSY WHIPPED. No, WHOOPED is a better description. Needless to say, it ultimately cost me my marriage.

When this whole affair came to light it was because it was too heavy for me to handle. I didn't know how to deal with falling for someone else while being married. It was killing me slowly. So, one night I just opened up and told my wife about it. And the initial suggestion was an annulment. But we never saw it through. We just continued to move forward until I went to jail.

And one day on a visit, my wife asked me if I was still planning to deal with this other woman when I came home, and I confirmed to her that I was. I really felt like I needed to at least give

74

that other situation a try in order to know if it was what I wanted. Boy was that the wrong fuckin' decision! She left the visit and the next time we talked she told me I'd be receiving the divorce papers by mail. She wanted nothing from me except my signature and for me to be a father to my son. Of course, she got both.

Make no mistake about it. Looking back as a mature man now, I know I had one of the best wives anyone could ever ask for. Before my son was conceived, she once told me that she loved me so much that if both our lives were at stake, she would die so I could live. To this day that statement fucks me up because I know beyond a shadow of a doubt, SHE MEANT IT! I've never had another like her since. And to be honest, I've accepted that most likely I never will. She's truly a "1 of 1". None before her. None to come.

I was released from prison June 2, 1999. And in a sense, it was bittersweet. I was happy to be home. My mom and my baby sister, Elesha, were there to pick me up. That was the sweet part. But I had to stay in Jersey on parole because they wouldn't allow me to be paroled to Philly. And it was bitter because after all the shit I put my wife through, losing my marriage, and no longer living with my son, I was being paroled to the woman's house I lost my wife over. And right before I was released, she told me she was now seeing someone else.

Immediately, the consequences of my decisions were coming back to bite me in the ass. This chick came within the width of a string of a horse's hair to leaving me in jail. The day I was in the counselor's office for them to call her to confirm the address is when she notified me of that seeing someone else bullshit. And that me coming to her house wouldn't be a good idea. I was able to have that conversation because the home plan counselor stepped away from her desk and allowed me to call shorty on the phone until she returned to speak to her personally. So, I was able to quickly plead with her. Saying, "Yo, if you say no, they're going to make me do the rest of my time 'cause they won't parole me to Philly." Reluctantly, she said, "Ok!"

But from that day forward, shit was never completely okay. And dealing with her was a constant uphill battle. And quite honestly, I deserved every step taken going up that hill. I blew the opportunity to have my son grow up in the same household as me. Something I, myself, didn't have either. But I never wavered or missed a beat as a dad. And now that my son is grown, I'm very thankful we have an amazing relationship because I know despite it all, he still loves me. But I also know that things could have been better had I made different decisions. I turned 30 and 31 while I was locked up. And once I was home, I was still growing as a young man. And doing my best to avoid the streets by working at jobs through temp agencies and oil refineries.

But of course, at some point, what you know and are accustomed to finds its way back to you. Especially when your closest friends are still gettin' money and livin' fast.

But the reason why my life after prison is so prevalent is because I never went back. Although I did get arrested on drug charges in January of 2006. Fortunately for me though, the police stole money from me and never showed up to any of the court hearings. Prompting the judge to apply "Nolle Prosequi," which means "No Prosecution." This resulted in the case being dismissed and I was free to go. That was a real blessing. Getting caught red handed in a car with nine ounces of cocaine and two pounds of weed, with a felony history wasn't a good look for ya boy. So those 2 weeks I sat in CFCF Correctional Facility were beyond stressful. My bail was $150K. And it couldn't get paid until proof was provided by the payor that the money existed in a bank account prior to my arrest.

It took my man "M" a week to find someone to do it. Which by that time my bail had gotten lowered to $75K. The process was called a Nebia Hearing. And once it was completed and approved, I was released. I was surprised those cops never showed up to court because they were some mean nasty muhfukkaz who I knew wanted to see me fall hard. They weren't pleased with my asshole responses to their threatening/condescending lines of questioning and suggestions at the time of my arrest. Especially when one told me, "We'll let you go if you give us the name of the person who's bigger than you." "You'll take these cuffs off me right now if I give you a name?" I asked. Knowing damn well he wouldn't. But fuck it. I had time to play. He said, "Well no, you'd still have to go through the system, but we'll release you later." I told him, "Oh Naah, ain't no deal!" And he got pissed.

My mother's address has always been on my driver's license. So, when the cops saw it, he said, "Is this where all the drugs and money are?" I told him, "No. I live there with my mother." He said, "We're going to this address and kick the door in. And whatever drugs we find, we're charging your mom with it. And charging her with conspiracy for what we found on you today. And she'll do at least five years. Can your mom do five years?" Now I don't know who the fuck he thought he was talking to, but I'm not a rookie in this street shit. Nor easily shook. I knew damn well they (a) were not traveling from Northeast Philly where I was arrested, to Southwest Philly where my mom lived, and (b) they damn sure wasn't charging her with the shit they just locked me up for. All bullshit talk to see if I was scared and would start "singing" like the lead singer in an RnB group. So, I looked this fool ass cop right in his eyes and said, "If you give her five years, I guess she'll be doing five years." He realized his antics

78

weren't working and slammed the door to the patty wagon in my face; as if to say, "Fuck me!" But in my mind, I was like, "Fuck You!" Cause his dumb ass had no clue that my ACTUAL address was less than four blocks from where they were arresting me. And there were seventeen bricks of "white girl" in a wall in my house, nine hundred pounds of weed, multiple handguns and an AK. That's why my address is never on my license. Those fools missed out on a promotion worthy bust. But fuck 'em (spits on the floor)! Their loss, not mine. I'm happy to have walked away completely with my freedom. My brother Derek used to ask me, "How the hell do you sleep in that house?" I was just numb to it. Never considered being robbed. Or had real concerns about the cops running up in there. I was just living and gettin' money. Plus, I was always low key and alone. No traffic at the crib. And it was super secure in there. My mind was on my main customers who were consistently coming up from VA to grab 75-80 pounds at a time. I had no time to think negative thoughts. I was thinking 'bout gettin' money. Not worrying 'bout gettin' caught. A few years ago, my man Def Ro (who I didn't know until "M" introduced us after I got out on bail) told me that he knew I had to be solid, cause once he saw all that shit in my house while I was locked up when him and "M" went to move it all, it was a reflection of what kind of friendship "M" and I have. Dudes not taking those kinda' risks for just anybody.

But anyway, back to my release from prison in '99.

Once I was released, those temp agency jobs I eluded to earlier were shared by my brother Derek. It just so happened that when I came home, he was released from Gratersford State Penitentiary in August of that year after doing 7.5 years. I introduced him to the sister of the girl I was living with in Camden. He eventually moved there from Philly too. At the time we were all we had. We still exercised outside together like we were in the yard. But we also job hunted together and kept each other grounded as we attempted to turn our lives around. Thankfully neither of us has gone back to prison.

Saying "I don't know" is better than saying what you don't know.

Chapter Eight
If It Ain't One Thing, It's Another

After about a two-year stint with the temporary jobs, I finally landed a permanent job at the Holiday Inn on City Line Avenue in Philly. Working there is when I learned that my personality was intimidating to some. Even my Supervisor. And not because I was doing anything wrong. But simply because of my "gift" to organically draw people to me and be a leader. I was even able to motivate my co-workers to move at a pace my manager couldn't. And when that happens, you mysteriously find yourself caught in situations beyond your control.

One night at work I was having an open conversation with two female co-workers. The conversation started with one of them referring to a female guest as a probable hooker. It led to that same person saying she was always interested in being a Call Girl in Vegas. So naturally at some point we're all talking about sexually related topics. But miraculously somehow, the very same girl who practically started the conversation, reported to management that I was having an inappropriate discussion and she felt sexually harassed.

Once my manager spoke to me about it, I felt like the odds were against me. And out of anger, I quit. I talked to one of my OG's, Mr. Lou Williams, and he said, "No, you don't quit your job! Go back tomorrow and rescind your resignation." So, I went back the following day and said, "Hey, I shouldn't have quit. I want to rescind my resignation and let you guys continue your investigation." Only to then be told, "Oh, I'm sorry, but once you quit there's no rehiring." It was obvious that I moved too quick and essentially had given them what they wanted. And there was no way to come back from it. I couldn't even collect unemployment because I quit instead of getting fired. But that's what was in the cards for my life at the time. And I took it.

From that day to this one, I have never punched another clock. I didn't know it then, but that was the beginning of me stepping out and really finding out what it meant to be creative in my life and turn things to my advantage. Which is another thing that has gotten me to where I am today.

There are still times where I did things my way. And learned from not listening. For some people like myself, it's necessary to learn that way. Otherwise you won't appreciate your journey in life.

So, some are going to make it through those hard times. While others will fail. And unfortunately, never recover. It just all depends on what life has laid out for you.

I'm sorry for those who end up having to go to prison; that's not a stop you want to make. I can say I never want to experience that again. Even though it wasn't a lot of time. It was still a combined 3 years too long, including parole. For me, double digit years wasn't necessary for me to learn the lesson I needed. And prison wasn't about being in fear. After a while I was used to it. It was about the inconvenience, disrespect, inhumane conditions, and loneliness that served as my deterrent not to return. Your relationships with family, significant others and the normal intricacies in life are all compromised. Even something as menial as going to the store when you feel like it will no longer be taken for granted upon returning home. Or at least it shouldn't. You can't dictate anything in prison. And you only have two options; get into the wrong mix and possibly increase your time. Or mind your business, do your bid and go home. At times the unfortunate occurs. And you just have to deal with those consequences when faced with them.

Despite all the arrests I've had over the years in Philly. When I got arrested in Jersey is when it resulted in me going away. To begin my 3-year sentence, I was assigned to Marlboro Camp in Central Jersey. There were no gates and no bars. It was set up like a dormitory. We had work details of picking up trash on the highway and painting. But once back at the camp, we could play basketball, softball, or walk around the big grassy yard out back. Sometimes we would just sit on the rocks in the wooded areas and talk shit. If you really wanted to, you could escape, but it wasn't worth it.

The worst part of being there was being away from my family and no woman to sleep with at night. But the conditions there weren't bad. Then an unexpected event occurred. One day as I was getting off the bus from my work detail and walking into the building, I was approached and stopped by two of the C.O.'s. They said I had to come with them. I always minded my business and was never in trouble. So, it was a shock to me and everyone else that I was being placed in a holding cell.

The C.O.'s was just as confused as me. Because they said they didn't know why, but an instruction to detain me had come from the head administrator's office. And the reason was simply, "it's an administrative hold due to an open investigation." And since I was in a minimum-security facility, I couldn't remain there while an open investigation lingered. Therefore, I had to be transferred to the maximum-security jail for that system, which was Rahway State Prison.

Once they were about to transfer me, I knew shit was about to be different. My ankles were shackled. And so was my waist, with the chains connected to the black box cuffs that stacked your hands vertically instead of horizontally. I suddenly felt like a real fuckin' criminal. And when I got to Rahway, I almost fainted. The only time I had seen that place was on the show *Scared Straight*. The energy was different, and the air was filled with confrontation and aggression. C.O.'s patrolling the halls at intake in full riot gear suggested that anything could happen at any time in that place. And they were prepared.

Since I wasn't sentenced to be housed in that facility, the only place to put me was in the "hole". Still stressing every second because remember, I still don't know why I'm there yet. Once situated in my cell, a whole week went by before I finally received clarity on who had administratively moved me. It was the Feds. They contacted the prison and informed them that I was a person of interest in an ongoing investigation. Causing me to be removed from Marlboro Camp.

Although I was relieved that I was finally aware of why I was moved. I was nervous as hell to find out what they wanted. But after seven days, and what felt like a loss of seven pounds later, a man and a lady agent came to see me. As they both got themselves situated at a table where we all sat across from one another, they got right into it. He sat a folder on the table first. Then a tape recorder. So strategic he was. As I was looking at the recorder, my thoughts were, "What the fuck do you think is going to happen with that?!" And then he proceeded to open the folder. Showing me a batch of income tax return checks. And asked me, "Do you know what these are?" I replied, "I don't know these people." He assured me that he was aware that I didn't know the people listed on the checks by name. But he wanted to know what I knew about the checks in general.

As soon as I saw those checks, I knew what they were and where I had gotten them from. And what I had done with them. But still, mum was the word. After he got tired of my charade, he grabbed the recorder and pressed play. And there I heard a familiar conversation between me and one of my homies. About those checks sitting in front of me, and some money I was trying to put together. See I wasn't the world's greatest hustler. And quite often there's been times where my friends who were great hustlers, put me in position to get money. I was always willing to take the same risks they took though, so it wasn't just me asking for money.

As I'm listening to the recording, my mind is racing 10 "thowzand" miles per hour. The primary thought being "how the fuck do I get around this?!" And secondly, "was this nigga wearing a wire, or was his phone tapped?!" I was wrestling with my thoughts. And I was stuck trying to figure out how they had our voices.

After he turned off the recorder, he looks at me and continued his dialogue. Telling me he knows who I gave the checks to. But he wanted to know where I got them from. I breathed an internal sigh of relief, at knowing there was information that they needed, but didn't have. So out came the mental chessboard. And when his questions kept running him into a brick wall, he finally said, "We'll be in touch," and left.

I thought that would be it and I would be returning back to where they ushered me in from. Days turned to weeks. Weeks turned to two months before I was finally released. Those bastards left me in the hole for eight weeks and I only got out because between me and my family calling the Ombudsman's Office, it was found that the Feds weren't holding me or charging me. I had just been sitting there stressed out and losing weight for nothing. Or really because the Feds said fuck me because their visit to me was non-assisting.

When I got out of the hole, I wasn't taken back to Marlboro Camp. I was taken to the medium-security facility, Rahway Camp. Right next door on the same grounds as the prison. Being in the hole was almost traumatizing. Watching how some dudes lost their minds from being confined was gut wrenching. Hearing dudes having sex late nights on the tier above me was worse. I heard slamming gates and jingling keys so much that when I finally was back on the streets, the sound of slamming doors or the sound of keys aggravated me. I was also very leery of being around people once I was home. I was always worried someone might do something to cause a reaction out of me that could violate my parole and I go back to jail.

So, I advise any and everybody to avoid having to go to the penitentiary at all costs. Pursue your dreams and your goals. Some people have dreams and aspirations of being the biggest hustler that ever lived. And if that's what you aspire to be, then rock out. Just be prepared for the repercussions. You quit. You die. Or you go to jail. Those are the escape routes, the only escape routes. And if you go to jail, make sure you take my homie from D.C., Spoon's advice, which is, "If you wanna be the best drug dealer. Also be the best inmate. Do your time and don't tell on nobody." Just accept the repercussions of your choices and decisions. Along with whatever life presents to you in that moment.

I often remind people that we only live one moment at a time. You're almost being too assuming or presumptuous to feel that you're guaranteed to make it through the entire day. Yet still you must pursue your aspirations confidently, and adamantly. With the understanding that just because you want something particular, doesn't mean it's meant for you. The best opportunity to be successful at obtaining our goals is to live a reflective life of what we want to achieve. Be kind to others. Especially the less fortunate. Always remain positive, knowing that whatever is meant for you will not escape you. But don't be mistaken. You do have to apply yourself in order to achieve success and receive blessings. God will guide your footsteps. But it's up to you to move your feet.

I provide that analogy when speaking to those who need to be motivated to excel. Including, and especially, with artists I work with in the music industry. More than anyone is AR MUZIC. Whom I consistently serve reminders by telling him, "Everyone thinks you're dope. But it doesn't matter if you don't think so yourself. You must believe in yourself more than anyone, no exceptions." Good thing he listens.

Unfortunately, however, there will be some people who fall short of reaching their desired positions in life. And they'll blame everyone except themselves. "Well I would have been this, but such an such hated on me." Or, "such an such wasn't trying to help," or, "I didn't have anybody to do this for me." That can't be your escape or excuse. You must take accountability for not being where you want to be in life.

At any time in our lives we find ourselves in difficult situations and we need a solution as to why. We must first look in the mirror and ask ourselves, "what did I do to contribute to this"?

Accountability is always a good formula to use when gathering an understanding about something that's going on in your life. There will be those times where things will occur that we just don't understand. And that's when you have to believe in the Ghaib (The Unseen) and have strong Iman (which is Faith); both Islamic terms. If you ask yourself that question and can hold yourself accountable for however you may have contributed to your own circumstances, whether good or bad, then that makes you a responsible person. These are character traits which are instrumental in becoming a well-rounded individual.

In predominant areas of this book, I'm obviously sharing personal experiences of my life and the results of my choices and decisions. Then there's moments where my intention is to motivate others on how to draw more successful conclusions in their own lives. The vernacular and dialogue may appear unorthodox at times. But that's because (if you know me) I'm writing pretty much exactly the way I speak.

The things I've experienced in my life are all relative to the motivation, inspiration and empowerment that I try to deliver to you guys because I'm only giving insight on how I've lived. Most times, my experiences are going to be relative to a lot of your life's experiences. And you can literally take pages from my book of life and apply it to yours.

I've heard on several occasions that I say what most people are thinking. Or that I've spoken life into them with something I said.

I don't have any special intellectual powers. But I do know that most people's lives travel a common course. And what separates people from one another is how they handle the outcomes of their respective experiences. We also need to consider that when we're discussing responsibility, it's not just for ourselves in most cases. This also applies to us for the children we bring into the world.

There are parents who find fault or displeasure within each other, causing them to inflict irresponsible behavior upon their children. Such as men who get upset if the child's mother is with a new man. Or angry because she'll no longer have sex with you. So now you won't take care of your child. Or women who are bitter because the man has a new woman and you won't allow him to see his child.

Parents who behave in this manner, whether they realize it or not, are adding to, if not creating, the detriment of their child's or children's well-being. Sometimes kids are too young to understand when their parents are being corny and petty towards one another. Causing the child to suffer. Because the behaviors they're witnessing are being internally documented by that child and could one day be repeated.

But there's also points reached when the child is old enough to notice what's going on and who's right or wrong between the parents. And you should be embarrassed if your child has to remind you of your immature actions. Being a responsible parent should always be the goal. Kids don't ask to be here. I personally have a 28-year-old daughter, whom I didn't know was mine until she was eight years old.

That's what happens when you have a wild and carefree summer at the age of 22. But once it was finally brought to my attention and confirmed years later, that she was in fact my daughter. I've been an involved dad from that day forward. Despite living in separate states. And once I made my mom and siblings aware of the new addition to the family, they embraced her as if she was a newborn. My mother actually saw her before I did. And she called me to say, "You ain't gotta take no test. This child is ours. She looks like you and your sister Erica." I don't know if my mom confirmed the test. Or if the test confirmed my mom. But they both were correct.

The older my daughter became, our interactions increased. And the connection was organic. Never forced and always pleasant. And as when my son does it, it always validates me personally as a good dad when my daughter calls me for advice. Or simply to check on me. Had I not played my role sufficiently, then those calls wouldn't take place.

If you've fathered a child, you don't have to be in a relationship with the mother in order to be an involved dad. And women, don't use the child as vices against men. You don't like his new girlfriend so therefore you don't want your child around "that bitch". Nah baby! As long as "that bitch" is not mistreating your child, or putting them in harm's way, or disrespecting you, you have to stand to the side and let "that bitch" be an adult while your child is in her presence. And men, don't let women make you think that they get to take you to the courthouse and put you in front of the Judge for what you don't do properly. If you're trying to be a father to your child and the mother is interfering with that, then you can take her to court as well. Don't use her actions as an excuse to abandon your responsibility.

Most of us were raised by people who taught us to do things the right way. Not too many of us were raised to do wrong or be disrespectful. Especially those with good parents and guardians. But at times, despite how we were raised we choose our own paths in life and make decisions that are against what we've been taught. And it manifests at times in parenting. The mothers and grandmothers of the old days raised children. Not just watched them grow up. And women cherished their babies. Remember my mom had me at 18. And when she was moving to Philly from Georgia the first time, I wasn't even

94

two years old. My grandmother wanted my mom to leave me with her. But my mom was not having it.

Today, it's not surprising when a child is left to be looked after by a person who's a family member of somebody the child's mother just met a week ago in a nightclub. Times have changed. But good, responsible parenting should never "play out".

Being real doesn't mean saying whatever comes to mind. Some of the greatest understandings were established through silence.

Chapter Nine
Georgia Boy

I wish I could have another laugh with my Grandmother. We always cracked each other up. Even when I was a child. I started this book while she was still alive. But we lost her on October 4, 2020. It wasn't easy watching her deteriorate from dementia. I cried years ago when she stopped remembering me. And I couldn't bring myself to attend her viewing or services. I didn't want that vision of her at all. So, I'll just cherish all the memories.

She once told me that when I was young, after she'd put me on the school bus and I got to my seat, even though I was too short to see out the window, she could still see my hand waving like crazy telling her "bye". She laughed like she was at a comedy show telling me that story. It was funny to her. My grandmother, or "Miss Louise" as everybody called her, worked in the cafeteria at the high school where my Uncle's and Aunt's attended. I always waited for her to get off work to bring home all the leftover goodies from that day's lunch.

My Grandmother really loved and cared for me. So much that she even got into an argument with her sister and did not speak to her for a while because she said I stole her car. But my cousin really gave me the keys to the car and my Grandmother was not trying to hear anything other than that. "He said she gave him the car and if that's what he said then that's what she did!" She really defended me and had my back.

One day I was playing recklessly, as usual, and I fell into a whole ant pile; red fire ants all over my body. I came running up the street, around the corner, screaming at the top of my lungs; I was about nine years old. She put me in a tub of bleach and water to wash the ants off me. Showing love, the way only a grandmother could do.

I have memories of those early mornings when my Grandfather (my Grandmother's husband) was getting ready for work and I would wake up to the smell of coffee, bacon and grits and toast. It's funny how nostalgia works. Because even as I write this, my nose is revisiting that familiar scent that filled my grandmother's house. But the highlight of the week was Friday afternoon at 3 o'clock when my Grandfather came home from work and gave us money for the store.

If you've experienced those times in your life you have to savor them. These are the people who shaped and molded most of us into who we are today. Or at least they played a major role in it.

My grandfather W.C. Hamilton was my dad's father. And I never understood the role he played in my life until he had already passed away and I was grown. I was too young to dig it as a kid. His house was positioned directly behind my grandmother's house. Only thing separating the two was an alley. So, in addition to whatever money I got from my grandmother's husband, or her, I'd also get from W.C.

I would go over there, sit in the house or out in his yard in those hard metal chairs that slid back and forth. Sort of like a rocker. And after a while of "visiting," he'd always pull out this blue change pouch in the shape of a football. He would squeeze the tips and the center opened up to an array of silver coins. Mainly quarters. He'd give me about a dollars' worth of quarters most times. And then I'd be off to the store. When I got old enough to reflect, I realized I was being a lil user. Most will say, "Oh you were just being a kid." And in essence I was. But looking back on it educated me on the importance of training your children to understand their actions. See my mom hated for us to ask people for money. She didn't play that. But that was the "You don't need no explanation" era. So, there was never a reason provided other than "because I said so". But had I known then what I know now, my approach may have been different.

The lesson learned was to be genuine, and sincere. Visit people out of care and concern. Not just because you want something. My grandfather probably loved having company at his age. And was genuinely happy that I was there. But he also wasn't a fool. So, he more than likely knew what time it was. And very aware that I was there to collect funds for my junk food escapades.

My mother has consistently told me, "As long as you live, you'll learn." And like everything else she taught that I listened to, she was right. I'm 52 and still learning. The longer I live the more I understand that statement. Because the more you seek knowledge and wisdom, you better your chances of succeeding in life.

I'm thankful I've lived long enough to apply what my mother taught me. And have been able to share those lessons with my children, siblings, other family members, friends and the general public. To keep them all sharp and on point. The best way to compliment your teacher is to equip others with what you've been taught. And it took me some time to accomplish that feat of maturity.

I wasn't always the influential person I am today. I once was easily influenced. Sometimes leading my own detriment. I had to transition and grow as a man into a space where I was comfortable making decisions that didn't follow the "wave". Eventually what I did and said became the influence. And with that comes responsibility. So, one has to be mindful of where and what they lead people towards.

Self-respect only comes from you.
You can't expect someone else to respect YOUR
SELF if you don't.

Chapter Ten
Home Team

Even though all my influences and role models basically were street dudes, some of them were also very smart and educated. My man Tommy (also known as Mu'Min) from Queens was one of them. It's ironic that I'm writing a book, but never have been an avid book reader. Muuk, as we also call him, was the first person that I can remember giving me books to read. I mean besides the Bible and watchtower magazines my mom presented me with. It was 1994, and Tommy and I were gettin' money together. But he was also into reading a lot. He's Muslim like me. But he also knows the Bible like he knows the Quran. I was actually impressed by his knowledge. One day at his house, he gave me a book called "Cop Shot". It was the story of New York Police Department Officer Edward Byrnes' murder, that took place in Queens. The book didn't have any mass appeal prompting me to read it, until Tommy revealed that most of the people the story was about or included, were from his neighborhood and he knew them.

So, him telling me all about Fat Cat, Pappy Mason, the Corley's family, and the legendary Supreme Team, just to name a few, prompted me to read that entire book. The way he told me about it made me read it. He also introduced me to the "The Art of War" by Sun Tzu and "The 48 Laws of Power".

Now I'll admit, Tommy was very animated. And I used to think he was fuckin' crazy when he was applying what he read in those books to the shit we were doing in the street. But a lot of times he was dead ass right. "The Art of War" taught tactics and strategies. 48 Laws gave insight on dealing with people individually. Especially in business. At least for me anyway.

So, this was another one of those friendships where even through some wild times and occurrences, I did learn something outside of the streets. I felt bad for him when I saw his friends Troy and E. Money Bags from Queens on the American Gangster TV show, after they had both been murdered. I met them when Tommy got married in Philly. So, to me it was crazy to watch their deaths broadcasted on television.

Like I said earlier, my life has to have purpose.

I've been around all kinds of potentially life-threatening situations based on my association that could have left me hurt or dead. And there's times I've participated in the harming of others. And could have been in jail forever.

After I came home from jail, I took a serious risk with my life and freedom. I was frustrated about not gettin' money. And wanted to get on my feet faster than it was happening. Either my man Big Dog or P.O. fronted me some weed, and I took it to Dayton, Ohio. I only knew one person in the whole city. And he was a fuckin' nobody. That should have been the only sign I needed to keep my ass home. But you know, a broke pocket overrides logic at times. So, I wrapped all that shit up, jumped on the Greyhound and I was out. I think I had two or three successful flips. Until the day I got caught slippin' and was set up to be robbed. I think this was my third time out there. I wasn't robbed at gunpoint, or anything physical. But the car I stored six pounds of weed in while I was getting my hair cut was, all of a sudden, mysteriously "stolen". Yeah, the car was gone. But it wasn't stolen. While I was gettin' a line up, I was literally gettin' *LINED UP*. And of course, once it was known that the weed was gone, it was obvious through body languages and lack of concern that I was being told without words, "Nigga you ain't from here and you're by yourself. What you wanna do?" So, I had to eat it. And my niggaz damn sure wasn't going to Ohio to go to war over six pounds of weed. Especially since I should have used better judgment about being there in the first place. That was some real dumb, broke shit I did.

And losing the weed could have been the least of my problems. When I got back and told Big Dog what happened, he told me I was lucky them niggaz ain't kill me. I never knew Ohio had a reputation for offin' niggaz. I learned a valuable lesson from that situation. Never place your safety and knowledge of your surroundings secondary to money. And I never did that shit again.

When I speak about the things we all go through in life, those experiences have lessons in them. The question is, will you learn from them and understand when it's time to turn the corner into a more productive direction? Sometimes you won't know when it's time to make a change. Unbeknownst to us at times; life will make the change for you.

Not too long after that arrest I had back in '06, shit started to get a little tricky. A truck coming into the city to bring us some "work" got pulled over, and the Mexican transporters were arrested, and the work was seized. We actually never recovered from that. So, you know how it goes at times in the game. Everything stops and it's every man for himself.

I had some bread put up, and I hit another lick for $32,000. So that would me hold me over a while. That was towards the end of '06. Then not long after that a guy I knew was shooting an independent film and made me the Linc Producer. We even used my house for some scenes. Gary Sturgis, Taral Hicks who played Keisha in Belly, Gillie Da Kid and Dutch from Major Figgaz along with Omillio Sparks from State Property were among the people in the movie. I actually had a role in it as well. This was around the Summer/Fall of '07. Most of that bread from months before was depleting. Living and spending with no real paper coming in was crucial.

After the movie wrapped, it was really time to make some changes. And my instincts of immediate survival kicked into overdrive. I needed money. Cause I was paying child support for my daughter and was completely involved with helping my son's mother with his expenses. I didn't care if I worked at McDonald's. Being broke wasn't an option. So, I started job hunting. Problem was I couldn't get hired anywhere.

I was well dressed. Tailor made suits. Nice shoes. Driving an E Class Benz. I'm not sure if the people didn't take me seriously, but no one would hire me. My friend Ros gave me a job picking up two kids from a school and dropping then off at her daycare for a hundred dollars a week. I did that for almost two months. Until I caught a blessing and "M" put me on to someone who needed a consultant for a hip-hop project. Which was right up my alley. We had just dismantled our label Colossal Entertainment, after putting out Omillio Sparks' solo album, The PayBack. But things didn't work out. So, we kept it moving. It was February '08, the new clients hired me, and it was on and poppin'.

After a couple months of working the project in the Northeast region, I decided Miami was a better location to market and promote the artist. It was May 2008 when I arrived in Miami. And I got right to work.

I never had my mind fixated on leaving Philly and moving because I couldn't fathom making a conscious decision to move completely away from my son.

But little did I know, being in Miami is what was best for me. And I believe all the blessings that were ahead of me, including now, were obtained. Despite my previous life of selling drugs and living fast. Once things became uncertain, I was humble enough to work at a day care and not allow my prior lifestyle to make me believe I was too good to endure a struggle. My life was just organically transitioning. I wasn't intuitive enough at the time to notice a change was necessary. Or maybe I did know but didn't have the courage to move. Inevitably, Allah designed it to where I had no choice. I was paying rent in Philly, but predominantly living in Miami. As if I was really gettin' money. But I wasn't. Not big money anyway. Everything just continued to work out. I really didn't want to leave Philly because that was my sanctuary. But since I was hardly ever there, I eventually moved my mom and her husband in, so rent wasn't continuing to be paid on a house that was rarely occupied.

107

Things continued to prosper in Miami. I had a girlfriend, Natalie, her daughter Isabella and our dog Lollipop. Essentially it was a ready-made family. It didn't work out with her, but things continued to transition, and it just made more and more sense to be in Miami.

When I got to Miami, I knew exactly two people prior to meeting Natalie. And that was a promoter and my man, Alex. Also known as Straight A, who transitioned from my friend to being my brother over the years.

I had fallen out of touch with Straight A and didn't have a good number for him when I got to Miami. I had met him about a year prior when we were there shooting a video for Omillio Sparks. We hit it off after standing on a street corner on South Beach talking for hours.

Once I was back in town, I felt bad that I couldn't get in touch with my guy. Instagram wasn't poppin' at the time so I couldn't hit him in the DM. But one day I was walking North on Ocean Drive, and this gray Ferrari came blaring down the block going South. I happened to do an over the shoulder look back to capture a second glance at that machine huggin' the strip. And on the license plate I saw "Str8 A". I was overcome with so much excitement that before I knew it, I turned and ran to catch him at the light. I know. It sounds a little groupie-ish. But fuck that! That was my nigga and I was happy. As anticipated, I caught him at the light.

He pulled over and we were right back in the mix of dialogue like we never left. He had his son with him, so we didn't talk long. But he said, "I'm 'a pick you up tonight and we're going out." I said, "Bet!" And that's what we did…FORTY-FIVE nights in a row after that. This was a different type of going out. Cause Straight A had a different type of "bag". He's the person who introduced me to Miami nightlife and helped me build my own network from how I carried myself and through his relationships. All the club promoters who fucked with him, eventually fucked with me. Respect was delivered in its highest form everywhere we went. Just as I was accustomed to from my younger years in life with Mohammed.

From the day we reconnected, we were inseparable. Although I was working and staying in a hotel and driving a rental, Straight A made sure his S550 and his drop top SL55 were both at my disposal. He also had a cigarette speedboat where we could be found almost every Sunday afternoon rolling through the waters of the Atlantic and Miami's Bay. His penthouse in downtown Brickell was at my convenient disposal as well. My loyalty and genuineness always put me in the best of company.

Through Straight I met some of my closest friends who became like brothers. Too many to name. But one of them was my nigga Prime. And our relationship flourished and lasted all the way up until he died. Almost twelve years later. From partying to the streets, our team was one of the most respected to ever do this shit. Our network expands all throughout the streets, the entire music, and entertainment industries. If there's an urban celebrity worth knowing, there's an 80% chance that in some capacity they're connected to someone in our clique. And any time they come to Miami; the alliances will be displayed. And it's not on some goofy shit. All respect, honor and friendships. A whole lotta money was spent on partying over a course of time from Dream on Saturday night with Jordan and Varsity. To LIV on Sunday with Mike and Phil from Headliner. This is partially what helped build and establish our reputations. All the rest came from who we were as individuals.

It was known and understood that we were cool and always out for a good time. But make no mistake about it, at a moment's notice we could go all the way left and be completely on the bullshit. And we didn't mind tearing up them people's clubs if necessary.

Two times come to mind where we had to show out. The first time we were in Club Play. I walked to the DJ booth to speak to Jermaine Dupri. And once I was done and headed back to the table, I saw a bouncer all in Prime's wife, Alani's face. So of course, I go over there to intervene cause no one else sees it but me at the moment. About 18 of us were there for Prime's birthday. I approached this King

Kong sized statue made of skin and bones, to find out what the issue was. He wasn't really acting like he wanted smoke until he saw he had the attention of a fellow bouncer. That's when he put his hands inside my collar, gripped me up and had my feet sliding side to side like I was on ice skates. He never threw a punch though. And I was in no position to. Straight A saw what was happening and soon as he saw a clean opportunity, BOOM, he hit that oversized stuffed animal right in the face with a magnum Ciroc bottle. Most of the dudes with us were all from Brooklyn. And we fought all those big niggaz 'til the cops came, pepper sprayed the whole club and shut the party down.

The other time is when me and Straight did the same shit at Karu and Y one night. But this time, it was just him and I fighting the bouncers. And no cap. They almost killed us. But let me back up a minute. I've never described Straight A. He's a country boy from Greenville, Mississippi. But half Irish. So, he's light skinned, and has a deep country accent. Tall and on the thin side, but not skinny. Super fly dude though. I said earlier he was gettin' a different type of bag. So, his entire wardrobe back then from the top to the bottom was all Gucci and Louis Vuitton. Shoes and sneakers included. But he also liked Prada sneakers. I started fuckin' my money up on more designer shit fuckin' with him.

By him being light skinned and well-dressed all the time (I mean button up shirts tucked in his slacks, belt matching the shoes), a lot of dudes concluded that he wasn't with the shit. Until it was always too late. Cause it takes less than the time to complete a good sneeze for him to be on go.

So back to Karu and Y. He had been out the week before and had words with a bouncer. I wasn't there. But he told me about it. And the following week we went back together. Not for confrontation, just to party. We had his girl with us at the time and his uncle. Straight and I left the table to go the men's room. And as we're walking back, him and the guy from the week prior made eye contact. They both won't look away. So, I knew where this was going. Straight said, "Oh you still wit' that bullshit from last week nigga?!" With his face and lips balled up and wrinkled like a discarded brown paper bag. As Straight starts his dialogue I was standing right next to him. We're all inches away from one another. I remove my sunglasses, and the dude looks right at me and asks, "What you takin' your glasses off for?" "Cause they're mine mothafukka!" was the reply.

He made the mistake of directing his attention to me and away from Straight. As we turn slightly to face each other, he jumps back into a karate stance. I said to myself, "Ahhhh shit, you 'bout to fight a black belt and get fucked up!" There was a wall behind me, but my back wasn't against the wall. However, since I was wearing a white shirt, and the wall was white. It appeared to Straight from his angle that my back was in fact against the wall. So, in his mind, the guy had me pinned against the wall, but he didn't. The dude never saw Straight take his ring and turn it around so that the diamonds were inside his fist. Nor did he see him take his bust down Rolex off. All this happened when the dude took his eyes off him. So, when dude was in the stance, and Straight thinking I'm subdued, BOOM!! He hits the guy across the face with a full bottle of Absolut Vodka he picked up from somebody's table. The bottle shattered, split dude shit, and caused liquor and glass to explode in my face and eyes. Cutting me on top of my head. Blood was everywhere. I couldn't see. So, when the bouncers came to help dude, they fucked us up. But hey, at least we didn't go to jail. I mean the cops came. But one of them was the brother of one of Straight's friends that ran the club. So, we were cool. Plus, dude didn't want to press charges. Some time went by and him and Straight ran into each other and it was all good. That shit was dead. We have a lifetime of stories. He was my homie then. He's my brother now.

When I was partying with Straight, I still had work to do for the artist that I was working with. I was on the verge of making this kid a star. But it just wasn't his time. Between him not being dedicated, and his investors reaching the point where they thought they knew more than me. It just turned goofy and no longer made sense to do. So, I continued my business with other clients and building my resume. I still however remained friends with my man Rha Sun, the kid's manager. I was happy that something I loved to do caused my organic migration to Miami.

The music industry and working with artists were my passions. Especially the developmental process. My greatest achievement to date is watching the progress I've made with AR MUZIC. A guy who once upon a time wouldn't even talk to anyone about the music business before I started working with him. He wouldn't even talk to the damn DJ's who we needed to play his records. I had to tell him, "Look Bro! If you don't talk to nobody, you gotta talk to the DJ's. In order to play your records, they need to know you and respect your grind." Yeah, well that took about two years. But eventually we crossed all hurdles. My network became his in addition to the relationships he established once he figured out how to be nice to people. He's a good dude. Just introverted and doesn't trust many people. And his level of genuine authenticity is so high that he literally doesn't understand how people live disloyally, or by being fake. I actually respected him from day one because when we were introduced as me being someone he should work with. He said he was in the middle of some personal things and would hit me when he was ready. Three months later he called. Seven years later, we're family now. And still working to develop his career and present his music to the masses. Although sometimes it seems like he should be a comedian.

My brother O.V., who I had been telling he should move to Miami, was on the elevator with AR and myself one day. And we always laugh at how AR deals with people. Or not deal with them. AR doesn't subscribe to a woman speaking to other men who are strangers while she's with her significant other. So, that day we were all in the elevator when a lady and a man got on. She spoke to everyone. And then they got off before us. AR assumed they were a couple and said, "Y'all see how she just spoke to us while she was with dude?" O.V. said, "She was just being polite." AR had a sincerely confused look on his face and said, "Well dammit, polite ain't right!" And we laughed at that fool for months after that.

In the summer of 2013, is when I finally convinced O.V. to move to Miami. I told him for years he needed to come. And when he finally did, it was a wrap. We grabbed a condo together downtown Miami on the 52nd floor, overlooking the Bay facing South Beach and the islands. At first, he was just here scoping everything out to get a feel for the transition. Once he saw how it was going down, and the type of team we had, it was a no brainer for him. My niggaz Gotti, Prime, Murda, Moose, "H," my man D from Albany, Rube, and the rest of the team from Brooklyn whenever they were in town, were just having it our way and on our time. Cuban Mike is another one of ours. But he's from Miami. And super certified.

O.V. immediately wanted to figure how to put a residual income in place. His idea was a limousine service, but just using sprinter vans. So, he arranged to have a custom white Mercedes sprinter shipped to Miami for us to rent out. Just to see how it would go. We even installed a stripper pole inside for additional entertainment. By then, I had been in Miami for five years and was comfortable with how I was movin'. Never leased or financed a car. I only drove rentals. Mainly because I could always switch up whenever I wanted. And my plug at the rental company always gave me whatever I wanted that was available.

But when "Mister gotta do everything on level 20" moved down here, he tells me in that low, slick, conniving Brooklyn mixed with Geechie tone of his, "Yo bro! I'm 'bout to turn up down here so you can't be driving no rentals. I know that's your thing and all. But we gotta make a statement." I tried to get around it, but he wasn't having it. So, after the Sprinter got here. We got our cars from New York and we had them shipped to Miami. He had the camouflage green Gran Turismo Maserati with the black wheels and red brake calipers. I had a S63 AMG Mercedes. Black on black. And I stayed stock on the wheels. It was a car show when we were all together at once. Prime had a yellow F430 Ferrari, then he had the red Ferrari 458 Italia. He actually had them both at the same time. Gotti had a black four door Aston Martin Rapide. AR was with by this time, and had a Maybach with his name on it. Straight A had gotten another Benz, a white CL63 AMG coupe. And that's just naming a few toys. We had a collective of other dudes we fucked with in Miami who added even more appeal to the campaign when they were with us. Needless to say, a hell of a statement and lasting impression was definitely made.

Even though "O" was back and forth to New York a lot, just having him with me felt good. We had experienced a lot together and separately over our 15 years and counting brotherhood. And this Miami ambience and change of scenery was very necessary.

I had his back. And he had mine. One time we found ourselves in a situation where we were all we had. A fight erupted in the club, Bamboo. Bamboo was our teams' "house". From the owners to the staff, we respectfully had our way in there. We even had our own assigned sections that were never sold unless we let the club know we wouldn't be out that night. My guys Dirty D, Purple, and Black Card Sia always held us down. One Sunday night, me and "O" were out by ourselves, chillin' at the owner's table with my man Theo Pasa. Some clown deemed it necessary to push me for talking to a chick I had known for a couple years, who also happened to be his girlfriend.

He was with Fat Joe and a whole host of Spanish cats from New York and Chicago. This dude didn't know me, nor my affiliations. Joe and the Terror Squad being among them. I just happened to be in a different area of the club that night.

After the guy pushed me, and I was keeping my balance to not fall, all those Spanish dudes rushed me like looters in the LA riots. They only did what was supposed to be done when shit pop with someone you're with. Only problem was I'm Joe's man. And he wasn't where the guys were who didn't know me. So, as me and "O" are fighting these dudes, Rich from the Terror Squad notices it was me. It was too late though. The melee was on. And by the time Rich, Joe, and the rest of his guys could get from where they were to me, to let his guys know that I'm one of them, the guys that ran the club who fuck with me had taken me and "O" outside.

This situation had UGLY written all over it. And everybody knew it. When you're angry and your adrenaline is moving faster than Andretti on the last lap, you say all the wrong shit out loud. "All y'all niggaz is dying TONIGHT!" I'm yelling while they're pulling me out the club. But in Real Nigga, true comrade fashion, Joe left the club, as he was celebrating his birthday and partying one last time before turning himself in to do that bid he had to do back then. He then came outside and around the corner where they had taken me, to assure me that he would handle it. And he asked that I not involve my guys who weren't there with me. Cause we're all connected through our respective cliques. Joe said, "I'm going to take care of the guy who pushed you and started all of this. But my other guys didn't know who you were. So, you can't blame them. And at least nobody cut your face, Bazz." Some shit the Terror Squad was historically notorious for. And that would have made shit worse. So, thank god that didn't happen.

I allowed Joe to handle it on the spot. Where he told dude in front of everyone, "You never put your hands on another man without an understanding. Especially over no bitch. Now get outta my sight!" And this clown didn't utter a word. Instead he walked away, head down and embarrassed. A couple of the guys from Chicago apologized like men. And I accepted. Because honestly, they only did what I, or any real dude in that situation would have done. They saw someone with them in a situation, and they responded accordingly. As they were supposed to.

After a few conversations with some of my folks in Miami, one of my Zoe's in particular, I found out this dude wasn't even a street nigga. He was a fuckin' music producer who was just affiliated with real niggaz and was showing off for the chick. I was mad all over again. But I still stopped Prime from sending a shooter to the video shoot we found out dude was at on South Beach one night. Because that was going to be messy, with police involved. Plus, I knew patience would present the right opportunity for retribution. So, I convinced Prime to chill. Because I wasn't trippin'. And then one afternoon just as I figured, opportunity presented itself.

I was alone one day on South Beach at South Beach Studios outside on the patio area. And the producer walks in without even noticing me sitting there. I gave him time to get inside before I walked in. And once I did, the staff immediately saw it in my eyes as I asked, "What room did he go into?"

When I was doing my homework on this guy, I asked someone to have him call me so I could try to put it to sleep with a verbal warning. But he had told them to tell me, "There was nothing to talk about." But once my Haitian man reached out to him and advised him and told him he should talk to me; he had the same arrogant response. Until he must have gotten tired of hearing that I was frequently inquiring about him. His concern led him to calling my Haitian man a couple days later and asking for my number. My man called me asking for the okay, and I told him, "Naah don't give him my number. Just like the message he sent me.... There's nothing to talk about. I'll see him in traffic!"

So now that it's just about to be me and him in this room, we're about to find out what all the tough guy shit really hit for. I told the studio staff not to let anyone in that room after they told me where he was. Reluctantly one of them said, "But Bazz, you can't do that here." The look I gave him suggested that he had just wasted words that could have been used for another conversation. I walked in the room, and as soon as he saw me, he said, "Yo! I was tryin' to get in t..." All he got out of his mouth was the T. Before he could release the "ouch" to say, "touch with you". I smacked the shit outta him. Sending his sunglasses into a crooked position from his face to the top of his head. And as we fought, he ended up in a choke hold with me telling him I'd break his fucking neck.

That's pretty much how the fight ended. And with me telling him he could have lost his life over some dumb shit. He apologized and I left. I felt way better approaching him on my own than having someone else do anything to him. In my opinion, approaching him alone was more gangsta and the best decision. And it materialized organically.

Sometimes listening to other people is effective. But at times, despite what others may think, you have to know what's best for you and know when to listen to yourself. Because you're the one who will have to live with the repercussions of your choices and decisions. And having to deal with discomfort or inconvenience because you listened to someone else only means you put yourself in that position.

Be comfortable after you've given your all.

You have no control over what the end result will be.

Chapter Eleven
Moment of Clarity

Now just because life moves in what feels to be a better direction, doesn't mean you won't be faced with challenges. Knowing how to "move" in, and adapt to any city I've ever lived in other than my own has always been to my advantage. And the most effective way of achieving that is to apply sound judgment, and create allies with respected natives of that city. And how you conduct yourself will determine how you're perceived. Or if you're worthy of being an affiliate.

Although I was stationed on South Beach for work, my actual and predominant work activity took place on what's called the "inland" of Miami. Or in layman's terms; the REAL Miami. Carol City, Little Haiti, and Opa Locka. I made friends in Liberty City, and Jackson's Soul Food Restaurant in Overtown was one of my favorite places to eat. Until my man Prime opened Prince J's Soul Food in Miami Gardens. In addition to the music project I was working on, I also had a small jewelry hustle where I sold to a few athletes and personal friends. My man Gino Pak from Milwaukee and his family owned a jewelry store there. The trusted bond we established is how I got into the jewelry game. They always kept me icy. One of our greatest moments of business was when Bleek arranged for me to introduce Gino and his brother J.D. to Jay and Beyonce on the Blueprint 3 Tour in Atlanta. They gifted Jay with a Rose Gold Limited Edition Breitling. It was 1 of 500 in the world. And a custom made 1 of 1 ring for Beyonce. That night is still a very memorable moment. Especially seeing Jay and O.G. Juan, who are both apparent watch collectors, laughing because when Juan saw the watch, he just smiled and said, "Oh, that's dope! But I already got that one." Despite wearing a lot of jewelry, and being in an unfamiliar city, and sometimes moving around alone, I still found myself comfortable around strangers who at any moment could have easily lined me up. But the way I carried myself is a testament to how I was able to get by with no pressure. Respect usually garnishes respect. Although there was one attempt to "press" me that occurred.

My man Rha Sun put me on to someone he trusted and knew, who said they had some folks in Miami who would hold me down since I didn't really know many people. I saw nothing wrong with it, so I allowed the introduction to be put in play. He gave one of the guys my number, the guy called, and I gave him a day and a location to meet me.

The day we met he showed up with about four or five guys. I was already outside so I could see them when they approached. Versus them already being in position and comfortable when I got there. The restaurant where we met had outside seating. And they found parking directly across the street. From a distance, I noticed one of them adjust his shirt and pants in a way that assured me had a hammer on him. The introductions ensued, we ordered food, had small talk about what I had going on and what brought me to Miami. Everything went pretty cool. I told them dinner was on me. And we left. In my mind I just met some aight guys that I may be able to form some type of allegiance with while I'm in town. Apparently, they had different plans.

The next day, the one who had my number called me. Very polite and cordial. His suggestion was that I speak with the investors of the project I was working on and let them know they should provide me with an additional budget for "security", so I'll be good while I'm in Miami. I listened and allowed him to almost complete his presentation until I peeped game and respectfully interjected. I informed him that I was well aware that their idea of "securing" dudes from out of town came with a price and stipulations I just wasn't willing to adhere to. "Nothing is going to happen to me unless God says so," I said. Adding, "I respect what y'all got going on. I got homies who be on the same type time. So, I'm not knocking your hustle." His response was, "Shabazz, you a real nigga! And I respect your position. Matter of fact, you're good in Miami regardless. If you ever have any problems, hit me or my cousin and we gotchu!" That was in 2008. As of present day, we call one another family. And I'm an honorary Zoe as far as they're concerned.

The cousin is actually who told the producer that I smacked that it was in his best interest to holla at me. Cause he knew I could have pushed whatever button I wanted to and get on that boy's neck. Thankfully, I don't just utilize the pressure I can apply frivolously. I don't want any of my dudes risking their lives and freedom on my behalf unnecessarily.

I created more alliances outside of my own squad along the way in Miami. Simply by being solid. Real Recognize Real is an accurate analogy in most scenarios.

I was pleased with how things were going for me. And being satisfied with your own efforts is a major plus towards growth and success.

Success to you doesn't have to be what's dictated by society. Such as cars, clothes, and other material possessions. For you, success could be the way you've established yourself and being noticed and respected for it. Or being content with comfortably providing stable living conditions for yourself and your family if you have one. For some people, being able to accomplish the above-mentioned responsibilities IS their success. They just don't understand it.

Too many people gauge their success against that of others. But everyone has to know how to accept the dynamics of their own life and allow those realities to materialize accordingly. I can't look at you and you can't look at me and say, "Hey, he's successful at that, so I'm going to be successful at it too." It may work that way, but it may not. How I did it may not work for you, how you did it may not work for me.

And everyone will not all be successful at the same ventures. So, find your niche and what works for you. If there's 10 pizzerias on one block, don't be the 11th. Open a burger joint instead.

When you're pursuing your aspirations and you happen to fall, those are your knees that get dirty. Not mine. When I fall, those are my elbows that get scraped up, not yours. We all have to accept our own life's circumstances as individuals. And continue positively towards what we say we want.

Some people might tell me, "Well yeah, Shabazz, that's easy for you to say". Because they feel I've "made it". When in all actuality, that's not necessarily the case and it's not easy to say the least. My life came with consequences. I've been through a lot to get where I am today, and it wasn't a smooth sail by any means. People tend to look at where you are in life now without knowing how you got there. They just see that you've arrived without seeing the journey.

I came up around a lot of people who were gettin' plenty of money in the street. And by me being in the music industry for so long, I've been around several athletes and entertainers. Some who've become friends or like family. When you're around people who have reached massive levels of success, and you want to be successful yourself, it's very easy to get sidetracked if you don't know how to focus on your own journey and understand what is, and what's not for you. At the same time mastering the art of knowing how to utilize your network to your advantage.

My life became better when I stopped worrying about tomorrow and accepted that all I have is right now.

Chapter Twelve
Here I Am

One of those close friends who is now like family is Allen Iverson. And he was well beyond inspiring.

I can't remember the first time we met. Maybe because the second time stood out so much. I was walking through Gotham nightclub in Philly one night. One of the hottest clubs in the city at the time. This was in '96. And suddenly someone jumps on my back, forcing me to give them a piggyback. I'm twisting and turning, trying to figure out who she was. Cause I was certain it was a woman. But nope! It was Allen. That was his way of greeting me. Ever since then we've been friends. And I love him now like a brother.   Bubba Chuck was inspiring in more ways than his ability to play ball or the flashiness he displayed from the wealth he amassed. Yeah, it was cool to be with him at Jacob the Jewelers and watch him spend $300K on jewelry. Or ride in his Benz's, Bentley's, or Rolls Royce's. Shit he was copping before other ball players and most rappers. But those aren't the things that made Chuck and I become friends. It was HIM. And it was ME. Us as men and individuals who grew up in the same type of struggles, but still valuing ourselves and family. And above all, caring about other people. I'll never forget sitting in that lonely ass cell in Rahway when I was in the hole. And I used to call his house collect. He was never there when I called. But his Aunt Lil Bit accepted the call every time. Just to tell me she'd let him know I called. When your family sees how you treat your friends, they'll treat them the same way more often than not.

The same type of rapport was built with Tracy "T Mac" McGrady. Another great friend turned brother. Mac's business savvy, in addition to the man he is, is what separated him from a lotta other dudes. I was talking to him one day in Prime's restaurant, and I asked him how it felt to have enough money to do whatever he wanted to do. His reply was, "Bazz, it's cool. But the biggest bonus is that my kid's kids won't have anything to worry about. And that's why I stay humble so I can keep receiving these blessings." I thought to myself, "that's some cold shit to be able to say". 'Bout a year or so ago he revealed to me that after the 15 years we've known each other, he appreciated my friendship because I've always been consistent and genuine. Never asking him for money and favors. I've just been his friend. And adopted his younger brothers Josh and Chance as my own.

When you're motivated by someone, it's important to not lose your own identity. I always make it a point to remain focused on what I'm pursuing and what's meant for me.

It was in 2003 that I started to get into party promoting with a then friend, who opened the door for me to do so. The first party we did was the Roc the Mic tour after party in Milwaukee. With Freeway, Fab, The Young Gunz and Memphis Bleek. At the time I wasn't aware that the foundation was being built for me to establish long term relationships within the music industry.

Friendships grew from those business relationships. All the above-mentioned guys became family. As did a host of others. From Meek to Trey, Puff and more.

Q. Parker from 112 is another person who I met doing business. But really became like a real little brother. We just don't have the same parents. And from my friendship with him, I've had the pleasure and experience of travelling extensively internationally working with the legendary group 112 as their Road Manager. This guy and I have the most outrageously funniest moments to last a lifetime. And one that I'll share is the time I had to take him and Freeway to Boston to host a party.

As I was about to pull off from Freeway's house, the cops pulled up behind us. Q is in the front passenger seat; Freeway was in the back. I'm driving. The cop approached and I already had the necessary documents before he got to the window. Free lived in a development at the time. And it was like 12-1 in the morning and we're getting on the road. So, the cops' concern was who lived there. Free informed him that he did. After he went to his car and came back, he still had questions. I had the door wide open. Leaned back with my foot and leg through the rolled down window with my elbow on the middle console.

And as I'm asking the cop why he is still holding me up, I see his eyes shift away from me and go around me. And he's saying, "Hey, what are you doing?" I look behind me and this nigga Q done got his scary ass out the truck with his hands up in the air. I said, "Yo, what the hell you doing? Getcho ass back in the truck". And he says, "Oh my bad. I'm from Georgia. We don't talk back to the police." The cop wanted to know where we were headed. And instead of asking him what difference it makes where we're headed. I politely told him, "That's Freeway, he's a rapper. And this is Q from the group 112. I'm taking them to Boston where they're both hosting a party together. The cop looks at Q with wide eyes after I said his name and the cop says, "Peaches and Cream?!" As the index finger pointed in excitement, "Aww man! Can I have your autograph for my girlfriend?" Now he dick eatin'. And he tells Free, "You know Beanie Siegel lives right around the corner. Hey, you think you can kick a lil somethin'?" Free told him, "Nah, I'm cool". And without further delay, we were on our way.

You never know what's going to happen while you're in a position of trust and authority when you're out with these artists. Their

134

lives, careers, and freedom for the most part is in your hands. Not a position for the faint hearted or the irresponsible.

A valuable lesson I've learned is to be very calculated when dealing with celebrities. The interaction can be tricky if you're not. You won't be respected or taken seriously if you don't know how to separate networking or simply socializing, from appearing star struck. You could easily be perceived as too "Joe Familiar" or a groupie. Something you never want on your quest to establishing yourself professionally.

No matter what you aspire to be. It's always to your advantage to just be yourself. Embrace your journey. You never know who's watching.

My friendship with The Champ, Floyd "Money" Mayweather is a testament of that. We didn't grow up together, we didn't meet in the street or in a club partying. We met after he saw something in me that he liked from observing my Instagram platform. His assistant Kitchie, who has already known me for years, facilitated us meeting at his request. And despite what anyone else's experiences or opinions may be about "Money" Mayweather, Floyd, the man himself, is undeniably one of the most solid and genuine people I've ever encountered.

Most people who have a problem with Floyd, in my opinion, don't really know him. Even when they see him in the media. They're still not seeing Floyd. The person they have a problem with is "Money Mayweather." The shit starter. The agitator. The one who deliberately gets under your skin like you're his opponent in the ring. The one who doesn't care what you think. Floyd is the family man. The one who does so much for black people undetected and out of the public eye that some would be ashamed of themselves for thinking anything otherwise. And to provide even more clarity. When people ask why he doesn't show his charitable efforts the way he shows off his jewelry, cars, clothes, planes and money. I say this on his behalf. Those are the things that are supposed to be shown. They're material gains accumulated from his hard work and dedication. And he's earned the right to brag after being poor and promising himself one day he'd live like he does.

The charity he gives SHOULD NOT be broadcasted. In his words, "Shabazz, I don't do things or help people to show off what I did. That's between me, God, and who I helped. Unless I decide to. Here and there." Anybody who doesn't understand that doesn't want to. They just rather be mad at a man that they don't know. Again, in my opinion.

I like to pride myself on walking with morals, values, integrity and principles. Trust, loyalty and consistency is my motto. When you carry those qualities, people will always notice you. Even if at times they don't tell you. Trust me, they're watching. We should all take this into consideration when pursuing our goals. The commitment of loyalty is owed to yourself first and foremost. Respect is to be given to yourself first as well. People will receive you as you present yourself. And you can't deliver those qualities to anyone else if you have yet to manifest them within yourself first. The results of all actions and encounters will begin with you. And if you're ever encountered with adversity, you still owe it to yourself to maintain your composure. Because how you respond will speak to your character. And know when to think twice. Thinking ahead is to your advantage. It prepares you for the unexpected. I always say I've never played chess on a chess board because I was too busy playing chess in real life.

Which brings me to where I am currently in life. As we search through life seeking our purpose, you'll find that your purpose just might find you. And you have to be prepared to embrace it and see it through. Because to deny it could mean remaining stagnant in life. And nonproductive.

Your purpose isn't necessarily what you want to do or what feels good to you at first. It's what you're MEANT to do. And could possibly take some adjusting and getting used to.

Over the course of my life, I've developed the skillset of being a listening ear to friends and family. And an honest voice of reasoning. It's who I am by nature and at my core. But never did I imagine that my own purpose would be to share this gift with the masses in a time where an entire culture is seeking strength, guidance and motivation. And I identify with it as purpose. Because I approached this responsibility blindly and not seeking finances or rewards. I simply delivered myself to you openly with transparency and authenticity.

January 4, 2015, I was in my hotel room in the Roppongi Hills section of Tokyo, Japan with my then girlfriend Nalini. She actually wasn't in the room during this historical moment. She was out somewhere with Alani, Karma and Lee. Prime, Gotti, AR and myself had taken the ladies to Tokyo for New Years. And it was also Gotti and Nalini's birthdays. So, I'm in the room alone staring out the window. I think me and her had just finished arguing before she left. I start scrolling through Instagram. I noticed the :15 second video feature. And I thought, "Hmmm, this is pretty cool." So, I figured out how to record and post. And did it. The first video I posted was about dudes who get it twisted and be mad at the other guy, when their

138

woman decides to cheat. And what I said in the video was, "Don't blame me. Blame the bitch!" I advised. "If I can bluff her, I can beat her. If she blink, she'll fuck."

I can admit for quite some time, the delivery in my postings, although very honest and real, was too abrasive and possibly offensive. So, I'm thankful that I had the wherewithal to curb that verbiage after realizing a lot of young, impressionable people, women and professionals, were acclimated to my page. Prompting me to shift the platform to a place of responsibility. I didn't want to be viewed as being "real and informative," but limited in my vocabulary because I cussed too much.

Things started to change immediately after I made a post about male groupies who damn near fight the females out of the section in the club so they themselves can stand next to or get a better glimpse of the male celebrities. My man Meek Mill reposted that video. And it went viral. I didn't know about it until I woke up to a text from my friend Michael Blackson, the African King of Comedy. "Have you been on your IG today?" he asked. "Nah, why?" I replied. He said, "Man, Meek reposted your video and your followers went up like crazy. But he said, "Next time, tell that modasucka to tag you." So, I went to my page and sure enough, I had over 6,000 followers. After having around 2800 the night before.

The more I posted, the more popular I became. The more popular I became, the more I realized the importance of what was happening. And one day as I was sitting on my bed, I had an epiphany. This was it. I recognized that my purpose had found me. My job is to help people by sharing my life's experiences and amassed wisdom and offer insight and warnings on how to navigate throughout this life. I jumped on the phone with Q and told him of my discovery and he was very encouraging and said to me, "Bazz, you've done something that a lot of people go their entire lives and die without doing." Referring to finding their purpose. The feeling I had was unexplainable.

But my next move was to create a foundation to build from. Something meaningful and relatable. So, I started my LLC and named it "Is It Worth My Life?" A question we should ask ourselves when faced with any moment where the wrong decision could alter our lives in a negative sense.

From there came the "Is It Worth My Life?" tour. Where I traveled to over fifteen schools, universities, institutions and radio stations. Morehouse University, Kennesaw State, North Carolina Central, Delaware State, a detention center for youths in St. Louis. And the list goes on and on. All of this stemming from primarily being the person my mother raised me to be. And being able to share that. After the transition from street life to a motivational platform, it was

140

encouraging to be embraced by supporters who consistently confirmed the importance of, and the need for what I was doing on social media. As well as what it does for them personally.

But just like anything in life. Where there is good, bad is packing its lunch to see where it can find a seat at the table of joy. I've unfortunately had to endure the ugliness of deceit and betrayal on this journey of bettering myself and others. Having Floyd as an openly vocal and visual supporter of what I'm doing, produced wolves in sheep's clothing. And no matter who you are, or what block raises you. We are all capable of trusting the wrong people. And some that I've trusted didn't value me or this purposeful mission. The interest was my TMT affiliation and personal agendas. So, after a great 2017 of traveling to places and speaking to a lot of kids and adults, 2018 proved to be the year of challenge.

I had to regroup because I found myself standing alone, with the exception of my new business partners, Maria and Crystal. Who had to assume the roles of holding my business together and halting the TMT Digital Network they initially came on board to establish with me. And to be honest, without those two, this whole shit would have fallen apart. But this is God engineered and 100% sucka proof. So, I never stopped posting, never stopped responding to DM's and comments. I never missed a beat. And no one ever knew I was in temporary despair. Cause I believed in what I was doing and paid attention to the signs. And embraced the blessings that continued to pour in even after going through bullshit. I never missed a meal. I still lived in a great condo with an amazing view. I had all I needed. And with the help of his mother, I was able to put my son through four years of college. All at the same damn time. Staying the course was the only option.

Imagine having renowned people in the world of music and entertainment encouraging you and telling you you're on the right path and to just not give up. My man Chop and Emory Jones were the first two people to let me know I was on to something huge. As long as I didn't quit. So, I continued forward. Even FLO-RIDA stopped me in the club one night, and urged "Keep doing what you're doing. All these industry dudes are watching you. Even if they don't comment. I know they're watching you. Because I'm watching". Those extra words of assurance were vital and much appreciated.

As I was relaxing at home one day, I got a text from my friend Sofi who was visiting from Chicago, telling me to come see her at the Mondrian on South Beach. Even with all the beautiful sunny days in Miami, I can still find solace being at home. But I got up and went. I suddenly had a taste for those lollipop wings and fries. Once I was there and after hanging out long enough to eat and talk a lil' shit, I was leaving to go home.

The eeriest thing happened after that. About two days prior, I was on a business call with a marketing company about doing some work for AR MUZIC. And in that conversation the guy was telling me about people he worked with and asked me if I knew James Lindsay who owns Rap Snacks. I said I know James Lindsay that used to work with Meek. But I haven't seen him in a couple years. He said, "Yeah, that's the same person." So, we carried on in conversation.

Back to the Mondrian. As I'm about to exit the pool area, who do I see? James Lindsay. I'm thinking, "Damn, this is a coincidence." But not more than what happened next. I walked up and spoke. We exchanged pleasantries. And I told him what happened just two days ago. He said, "That's crazy I'm seeing you because I've been watching your Instagram and you're killing that shit. And I've been wondering if you've monetized your platform." I told him I had not. And he said, "You need to come to my office tomorrow so we can talk and put some things together for you."

That was October 21, 2018. And from that first meeting, my Electronic Press Kit was created at his request by someone he works with. He immediately began sharing all his thoughts he'd compiled while watching me build this platform. Work was being put in from day one. And he always told me how far I could go, and what bounds I could leap. And his philosophy about money? 'Cause I'm thinking to myself, "shit I gotta pay this man". "Shabazz just keep doing what you do. I'll do what I do. The money gon' come. Don't worry about that." Is what he said. For once, besides Maria and Crystal, some real shit had arrived. Sitting in his penthouse office overlooking downtown Miami, I could feel the paradigm shift. All I need now is for Maria, who is my business partner and manager, to hear his plans and agree. And that's the scary part. She is literally a boardroom bully. Can't let that ponytail and peep toe shoes fool you. She's all the way about her business. And super protective of me. So, if all this shit I'm excited about don't sound right to her, then I'm back to square one. So, we arranged a meeting for her to fly into Miami to meet James and other staff regarding the podcast and overall branding intentions for me. That was January 2019.

The whole time I'm thinking, "Please Maria, don't be mean to these people." But after hearing them out, she started talking. Then she asked questions. Then engaged in full blown conversation. And then I knew it was all good. She does not engage in extended dialogue if she's not feeling the direction the conversation is going in. She'll listen and allow you to talk through your entire presentation, and then simply say, "Thank you, I'll be in touch." After she said everything

144

was all good, the only thing we needed now was a contract to be produced, to consummate what we discussed. And move forward. We hadn't arrived at success yet. But dammit I felt we'd been invited, and figuratively at home getting dressed to go.

The plan was practically coming together on its own. And opportunities continue to manifest. As I look back over all the years of tests, trials, bad decisions, poor choices and sad times, there's not much I would take back. Minus the people I love whom I've lost to death. All of my experiences were necessary for me to be who I am, and to be equipped to deliver this dialogue the way I do.

I'm thankful that I've lived life long enough to determine what's really important. No matter how much money or wealth you've accumulated, life is about GIVING. And sharing with those less fortunate who would never have opportunities to experience certain delicacies in life unless someone shared with them. There's a different type of appreciation I have for life and the people in it. The animals, the scenery, and the infinite creations we get to enjoy.

All the things that I DID NOT DO, because I thought I'd go to jail for a thousand years or lose my life in the street was all healthy paranoia. That kept me from going too far to turn it all around. Thankfully I was being preserved for this time in my life. There was always something greater lying ahead for me. Even when I didn't know it. And that "something" was an opportunity to share a lot of my

experiences in an effort to help you FLIP *YA LIFE*.

Talking positive doesn't suggest that you're perfect. It just means that despite your flaws you still choose to be better.

Moving the Culture Forward

How to move the black culture forward while continuing to follow established agendas that keeps us oppressed, has become more commonly the most important question or conversation in many rooms and on multiple forums. I've heard some say, "We have no culture." And shit, I'm smart enough to know better than to argue with those people. Cause it's possible we're using the term to replace the lack of a more befitting one. But for certain, the circumstances surrounding the word is real. And the conversation is needed.

When asked, "How do we push the culture forward OG?" I simply respond consistently with one word, "ACCOUNTABILITY." Period. Point blank. That's it.

Some seem to believe in this magical procedure where we all collectively make the necessary adjustments or changes at the same time. Or at least on command. It's unfortunate to say, but that's just not going to happen.

No matter how many more atrocities we witness, or marches that are orchestrated with emotionally driven crowd participation. Nothing will change or go forward in this, or ANY culture faced with challenges that require emergency responses, unless people become responsible and accountable for their own actions.

Too often, when people speak out against current conditions plaguing our culture, the general consensus seems to be that it's deemed appropriate to announce to everyone besides ourselves what needs to happen to achieve the cultural success we claim to desire.

Through loud voices, social media posts, or bullhorns, we repeatedly hear "WE have to do better. WE have to stick together. WE have to support one another." But somehow, historically the dialogue always comes down to an argument or disagreement because one person is telling another what THEY should do differently.

WE should translate to US. Not ME amplifying YOU and your faults and flaws. Change will come about organically if people would simply BE THE CHANGE, THEY SAY THEY WANT TO SEE. I'm not sure how to simplify this analogy.

Effective change starts in the mirror.

Another way of driving us forward is to establish a more constructive form of communication between ourselves. And especially with law enforcement.

I'll start with policing. There's no definitive way to rehabilitate the downtrodden relationships between police and the black community. Training isn't the issue. Nor is it the lack thereof. Impulse, cowardice, and fear are what's plaguing those officers into poor choices and decision making. A vast majority of police related

· incidents and killings are the result of what an officer CHOSE to do. And legislation is designed to uphold and support those ill-advised choices.

But again, it goes back to accountability. Cops who WANT to have better community relations with residents, WILL. Cops who do not want to kill an unarmed, non-threatening person, simply WILL NOT.

We, as citizens, also carry a level of responsibility regarding how we deal with police officers. There are plenty of times, and will be more to come, where the cop is wrong, and we are right. But, try to remember. There are ways to conduct yourself. Even when you're in the right.

We have to know how to get our points across, and create teachable moments, while defending ourselves all at once. It requires the skill of finesse. So that's a trait you should work on adapting if it's not already in your repertoire. It's imminent to remember that although we may be standing within the parameters of lawfulness. How we respond to unprofessional police behavior at times will dictate the direction of the interaction. Always try to be the one in control. And that's done by not relinquishing your emotions to your opposition. For example. If you're approached by a cop who's being aggressive or disrespectful. You would be behooved to NOT

RETURN THE SENTIMENT. Instead, place your pride aside, and you be polite. The objective is to leave the scene not in handcuffs, in an ambulance, or in a van to the morgue. The respectful approach doesn't always work. Because if a cop has his or her mind made up to be an asshole, and ultimately arrest you. That's EXACTLY what they're going to do. Fighting, and trying to put up a defense only gives them reason to harm you and LIE about it. The only way, and time to deal with it at that point is legally, and later. And don't allow some hyped-up lame to gas you up about what they would do if it was them. Because all they'd be doing is giving you a recipe to die or go to jail.

Those brief examples are just a couple of many to be discussed as it relates to our personal advancement, and sometimes for our personal safety.

So in closing, I implore us all to not neglect the importance of effective parenting. That's where the culture begins. How we raise our children, a high percentage of the time, will dictate what type of adults they'll become. We have to be PARENTS. Not HOMIES and GIRLFRIENDS. If you instill certain morals and values into your children or your child, even if they grow up and stray from the path you taught, at some point, remnants of those teachings and lessons will manifest themselves and provoke thought.

One of my most enriching moments as a father (besides my children growing up to be awesome) was when I asked my son one day who he looked up to among the athletes and entertainers he likes. His response was, "I don't look up to anyone except you and mommy." At that moment it was confirmed to me that I was effectively performing my duties as a dad.

Raise your children. Don't just allow them to grow up. And once they're out on their own, no matter what decisions they make, always be able to look yourself in the mirror and say, "I'm proud of what I did."

A Letter to Prime

 Tuesday, January 15, 2019, you FaceTimed me and you said, "Wus poppin' Chali. Where ya at?" I can hear your voice as I write this through tears. You of all people know being in the house was my new thing. It started costing too much money to be outside. But you're never to be denied. So, I met you on South Beach at Oceans Ten.

When I walked up, you were sitting there with two friends and you introduced them to me saying, "This is my man, my brother Shabazz. He's Shabazz The OG on Instagram. Y'all gotta make sure you follow him. He be talkin' that shit!!" Your smile and sincerity were as if you were talking about yourself. But that was you at your core. A good dude who applauded others. And who would ride on four flats for who you loved.

Over the course of eleven plus years, we've argued twice. Both times I thought, "Damn, I hope I don't have to fight this crazy mothafukka. Cause he gon' fight me like a stranger. And I don't know if I want that." But every other time has been nothing but brotherly love.

That January day you wore an off-white hoodie that I had my eye on. And I told you, "Today is your last time wearing that. I'm taking it cause you ain't gonna wear it again." You said, "You got it Chali. I don't want no smoke."

When we were done eating, I told you I was going to Vegas on Thursday to go to the fight with Floyd on Saturday. I asked you if you were coming. You said, "I'm going to LA today and if I come to Vegas, I'll let you know."

We parted ways at that point with our customary exchange of "Love you bro. Love you too." I know I said it was your last time wearing the hoodie. But damn Prime, it wasn't supposed to literally be your last time my nigga. And on top of it, you did go to Vegas on Saturday with Rugs and you forgot to call me. And I left that following Monday night not knowing you were already there in the hospital since Monday afternoon.

Gotti called me Tuesday morning as soon as I walked in my crib. And it made my knees buckle to hear him say, "Bazz where you been, I was calling your phone all night. Prime just had emergency brain surgery in Vegas and it's not looking good." I'm wondering, "How?" I mean I'm literally walking in the door from Vegas. I was sick. I couldn't even leave that day. The next morning, I was back out on the first flight.

I can't help but wonder if I would have been with you when everything happened, would the outcome have been the same. I was always there whenever you needed me. Like the time you were outta town and called me in the middle of the night because Coca thought someone was breaking in. And I drove all the way to Miramar, only for it to be a got damn raccoon. Or when yo crazy ass had me and Gotti meet you by Star Island in a damn uber, and you were on a jet ski 'cause you wanted the hammer to go look for some dudes who used their jet ski's to splash water up onto your boat. Those are just two times out of many, where we were side by side. Damn! Where was I this time? I mean don't worry dawg; I'm not blaming myself. These are just my thoughts. Thoughts that create too many questions that'll never be answered. Can't front though bro, me and the boys are fucked up over this one. And I just wish I was with you, at the time this shit happened.

AR changed the color on the Ferrari to the red that you had on yours. And called it PRIME TYME. Then later made it a race car. You know he gets bored easily with those cars.

Shy Glizzy put a song out about you, and he titled it "Prime Tyme".

Rah got your face tatted on his back.

Gotti got some mean diamond dog tags made that the Pristine Boyz did for him. Your face on one. And the other with your favorite saying. "Til Death Do Us Part. We All We Got."

The whole time you were in the hospital, we all were there with you. Holding Coca down. Rube was there 'til the final moment of clarity. I know he'll never be the same.

Majesty is bad as hell. And crazy just like you. Oh, I had to pop him on his ass one night for hittin' Coca. I know you didn't do physical discipline. But I had to let him know that hitting his mom was never going to fly.

Prince is the smartest kid in the universe. All he does is make straight A's in everything. All so he can have a reason to get money for those damn gift cards.

Coca Lani is still a soldier. Those boys couldn't get a better mother if good mothers were on sale at the mall. Simply put, she's the shit. And you'd be proud.

Miami ain't the same without you. My eyes tear up every time I go to places, we frequented. Or whenever we're on the yachts. And forget being in the club. Your presence is always there for sure. Headliner made sure they gave you a tribute at LIV on Sunday. The day after we laid you down for good. It's crazy cause Nipsey was there that night and Breyon insisted that I meet him. After I did, I felt like he was a good dude. Unfortunately, along with your man Cliff, within the next 30 days they'd both be gone. Life was looking very somber all of a sudden. Or as we would say, "looking real spooky".

It was a bittersweet night at LIV. But we pulled it off. Brooklyn held you down. And your image was on the screens all night.

I told you about the book, but you didn't make it to see the completion. So, it wouldn't be us if I didn't include you in it. Anybody who didn't know before, found out after you left that the boy Hollywood Prime Tyme from East New York in Brooklyn, was official like a referee whistle. Ya hear me?! One last "SU WOO".

I Love You, Bro! #PrimeTymeForever

Conclusion

I graduated high school with a little over a C average and didn't attend college. But in no way does that equate to a lack of intelligence.

There will come times when it's necessary to perform tasks that quite frankly may not make sense to us. But due to not being in a position of power or authority to do otherwise, we have to exercise adherence. And recognizing this is imperative.

This is where decision making can become a challenge for many. And some may conclude that life is hard. But in essence, it really isn't. In my opinion.

We all face difficult moments. But the complexity level of those moments depends on our ability to make sound decisions, and how we approach conflict. That's what determines if life at the time will be hard. We control it.

For example, when negativity arrives, it doesn't mean it's automatically welcomed. It's like an unwanted guest knocking on your door. They will not get in unless you invite them. So, when a situation presents itself to you that may potentially make your life difficult, use your ability to control your space with the decision to welcome it into your life or not. Always have personal insight and acceptance of what's beyond your control. Sometimes WE make life hard by attempting to see a circumstance the way we'd like it to be instead of for what it really is. Acknowledge and execute. Identify and rectify. That's how we should navigate through life.

If shit goes wrong, fix it immediately no matter what it is. Give it no time to fester or marinate. The choice to do so or not will dictate certain results.

That's what this is about, choices and decisions.

Do we always make the best ones? Of course not!

I've discussed divorce, prison, and being in the streets among other things. But the above mentioned are what helped develop the man I am today. Learning those lessons through experience is why I'm able to speak to you guys the way that I am. Allow my life to be your reference boards.

A Smart Man Learns from His Own Mistakes. A Wise Man Learns from The Mistakes of Other's.

The dopest part of sharing your life story with someone is hoping you'll make theirs better. When you give bits and pieces of yours, you have to make your experiences so transparent that the people feel like they are walking in your shoes. And that's what I try to deliver. I want you all to feel me because this shit is real.

Before I exit, I simply ask this of you all. If you take nothing else from this book, at the very least leave with this … An in-depth understanding of the importance of holding YOURSELF ACCOUNTABLE for your own actions. So many people say they want to see change in the world and our culture. But they want to change everyone else and not examine themselves. Be the change that you say you want to see. Because the mirror is where the world starts its change.